Margaret Cooling is the author of over 40 books on RE and a:
books for churches. For many years her speciality has been ir
communicate Christianity within the field of education, and she
number of publishers, including the National Gallery Company and the BBC.
Margaret has taught in both primary and secondary schools, and for the last 20 years
she has been engaged in writing and training across the UK. She trains both teachers
and clergy to work in schools. In the past few years Margaret has begun to adapt her
experience and knowledge within the field of education to work with churches.

Important information

Photocopying permission

The right to photocopy material in *Bible Storybags®* is granted for the pages that
contain the photocopying clause: Reproduced with permission from *Bible
Storybags®* published by BRF 2011 (ISBN 978 0 85746 073 8), so long as
reproduction is for use in a teaching situation by the original purchaser. The right
to photocopy material is not granted for anyone other than the original purchaser
without written permission from BRF.

The Copyright Licensing Agency (CLA)

If you are resident in the UK and you have a photocopying licence with the
Copyright Licensing Agency (CLA) please check the terms of your licence. If your
photocopying request falls within the terms of your licence, you may proceed
without seeking further permission. If your request exceeds the terms of your CLA
licence, please contact the CLA directly with your request. Copyright Licensing
Agency, 90 Tottenham Court Rd, London W1T 4LP. Tel 020 7631 5555, fax 020 7631
5500, email cla@cla.co.uk; web www.cla.co.uk. The CLA will provide photocopying
authorization and royalty fee information on behalf of BRF.

BRF is a Registered Charity (No. 233280)

Text copyright © Margaret Cooling 2008
Illustrations copyright © Ann Kronheimer 2008
The author asserts the moral right
to be identified as the author of this work

Published by
The Bible Reading Fellowship
15 The Chambers, Vineyard
Abingdon, OX14 3FE
Tel: +44 (0)1865 319700
Email: enquiries@brf.org.uk
Website: www.brf.org.uk
BRF is a Registered Charity

ISBN 978 0 85746 073 8
First published 2008
This edition 2011
10 9 8 7 6 5 4 3 2 1 0
All rights reserved

Acknowledgments

Unless otherwise stated, scripture quotations are taken from the Contemporary English Version of the Bible published by HarperCollins Publishers, copyright © 1991, 1992, 1995 American Bible Society.

Scripture quotations from The Revised Standard Version of the Bible, copyright © 1946, 1952, 1971 by the Division of Christian Education of the National Council of the Churches of Christ in the United States of America, are used by permission. All rights reserved.

Storybag® and Storysack® are registered trademarks of Storysack Ltd. The term Storybag® is used in this book under licence and may not be applied in any other context without prior written authorisation from the registered trademark holder.

Performance and copyright

The right to perform *Bible Storybags*® drama material is included in the purchase price, so long as the performance is in an amateur context, for instance in church services, schools or holiday club venues. Where any charge is made to audiences, written permission must be obtained from the author, who can be contacted through the publishers. A fee or royalties may be payable for the right to perform the script in that context.

A catalogue record for this book is available from the British Library

Printed by Lightning Source

Bible Storybags®

Reflective storytelling for primary
RE and assemblies

Margaret Cooling

To Doris Males, my mother, who is 80 this year.

Acknowledgments

I would like to thank Doris Males for the pattern for the knitted figure and the ladies of St Mark's Church, Cheltenham, who knitted dozens of figures along with Doris Males and Jean Dangerfield. I am also grateful to Terence Cooling for creating the interactive website and the following people for their help in trialling these stories:

Mary Myatt
Karen Metcalf
Ania Canon
Sue Hookway
Carol Henderson
Marguerite Budden
Christine Christian
Marian Carter
Mary Payne
Katie Orchard
Carol Macdonald
Clare Sanders
Gill Green
Sandra Pollerman
Fiona Knapp
Helen Mitchell
Mary Carter
Mary Lewis
Catherine Todd
Jill Walker
Students of the University of Gloucestershire
Children of Ernehale Infant school, Arnold, Nottingham
Children of St Mark's C of E Junior school, Cheltenham

Contents

Foreword

Bible stories deal with the big issues of life: love and faith, hope and despair, life and death. They are stories that engage with the big questions: 'Who am I?' 'What is important in life?' 'What is God like?' Unfortunately, for many children (and adults), the ancient and much-loved stories of the Bible appear irrelevant in their everyday lives. However, when invited to engage with the Bible fully, in an imaginative and meaningful way, children find that not only do the stories come to life, they can even be life-changing. Bible stories can be the vehicle that stimulates thinking, feeling and creativity, helping pupils to engage with key questions of life and express their own views in response.

Reflective storytelling is a vehicle that allows children to engage in a conversation with the Bible in a new and exciting way, which reflects their own thinking and personal learning styles. Well presented, a reflective Bible story will not only help the listeners to understand the Bible, it will free them to wonder: 'What would I have done if that had been me?' 'Perhaps I need to think some more about…' 'Do I agree when…?'

In this book, Margaret Cooling offers a variety of stimulating approaches to reflective storytelling, which can be used in primary school RE or collective worship. Teachers will easily be able to access these approaches at a level and in a manner that is most appropriate to their own school situation, and embed them in their school's syllabus.

Use this book to give your children the gift of reflecting, but remember that thoughtful and reflective imagining takes time—and can last a lifetime. Ultimately, the best judges of the effectiveness of this book will not be you or me, but the children who have been given the tools to open up the Bible for themselves.

Dr Shirley Hall, RE Advisor for Schools, Diocese of Ely

Introduction

The scripts in this book can be used in RE or assembly (Collective Worship / Religious Observance). In an assembly context, use a table so that all can see, or use a screen or whiteboard and the interactive website (see page 10). Make sure you lift items high before placing them on the cloth.

The book uses methods designed to stimulate both thinking and feeling—the creative and the cognitive.

In the scripts, meaning is conveyed by the rhythm of the language, the gestures, the objects and many 'cues' that the mind picks up intuitively. By the end of a story, children might feel they know what it means without being able to put their understanding into words. The biblical story and follow-up work often clarify what has been grasped intuitively. With this approach, there is room for the children's ideas concerning the meaning of the stories and space for them to share the Christian community's understandings.

The colour of the storybag® and many of the objects used are symbolic. The road often symbolizes a person's journey through life. Teachers can follow up these symbols or leave them without comment, depending on the age and aptitude of the pupils.

Learning from religion (Personal search): fulfilling the requirements

The approach used in this book enables teachers to deliver both attainment targets—'Learning about religion' and 'Learning from religion'—as indicated in the Non-Statutory National Framework for Religious Education. It is particularly strong on 'Learning from religion'—the part of RE that many teachers find most difficult. 'Learning from religion' is concerned with identity, experience, values, commitments, purpose, meaning and truth. It is about encouraging pupils to reflect, ask questions, interpret, apply, evaluate and express their own understandings. In Scotland, much of what comes under 'Learning from religion' is found under the heading 'Personal search'. It is important in 'Learning from religion' and reflective RE that activities should not be intrusive. Keep questions general: for example, ask, 'What type of things do people say sorry for?'

The assembly material in this book enables teachers to fulfil the law concerning collective worship (*1988 Education Reform Act*) in a way that is participative, as encouraged by circular 1/94. It can also help teachers in Scotland to fulfil the legislative requirements on Religious Observance (2004) and circular 1/2005, as it focuses on the reflective element and includes mystery, values, meaning, 'otherness' and challenge.

The book can be used as stimulus material for developing the five thinking skills (see page 11) listed in National Curriculum 2000.

Prayers and reflections are provided for teachers to use as appropriate. Pupils can be invited to participate in these elements but should not feel that they have to.

Access for all

There are two scripts for each story, one suitable for younger pupils (4–7s) and one suitable for older pupils (7–11s). The scripts can be used in faith-based schools and community schools. Teachers will need to select from the follow-up material according to the age and ability of their pupils and their context. The methods used give access to pupils of all abilities, as different ways of knowing are used (intuitive, symbolic, reasoning and so on), and the physical and visual nature of the stories makes them particularly suitable for many children with special needs. The scripts have been designed so that pupils can learn at different levels; the meanings are layered so that gifted and talented pupils can dig deeper into the symbolism and ideas.

Introducing and sharing Bible stories

Biblical stories can be introduced and shared with pupils using a form of words that earth them in the Christian tradition: for example, 'Today we are having a story that is important for Christians' or 'Today's story comes from the sacred book of the Christians, the Bible.'

This leaves the pupil free to identify with the story or not. They can respond with 'That's my story; we read that at home / in my church' or 'Now I know why that is important for Christians.' It is important that pupils feel free to make their own response to the story, as long as it is respectful.

The scripts are deliberately ambiguous and relate to a biblical story without being that story. This stimulates curiosity—the basis for learning. They are designed to create conversation and discussion, encouraging the pupils to share their own ideas, and to be interactive. Different ways of using the scripts in an interactive manner can be found on page 12.

Pupils can become 'RE detectives' in order to work out what the script is about and how it relates to the biblical text. Packages such as 'WordArt' can be used to create badges, or you can photocopy the templates on this page.

The material in this book draws on insights from many areas: story sacks®, thinking skills, brain-based learning, Christian spirituality, Godly Play, the use of the creative arts, spiritual development and faith development. Each script is, however, original.

The scripts may be photocopied for use within the purchasing institution only.

Websites

Some websites are indicated as sources for extra information or images. Generally, images can be found by using Google—typing in the subject and then clicking on 'images'. NB: Please check copyright on all websites before downloading any material. Please also note that websites do not necessarily reflect the views of this author.

Health and safety

All activities should be carried out with due regard to health and safety. Teachers are referred to their health and safety document.

Reproduced with permission from *Bible Storybags*® published by BRF 2011 (978 0 85746 073 8) www.barnabasinschools.org.uk

Using the storybags® in RE and assembly

Select a story script appropriate for the age of your pupils. You can either use the script (followed by a few questions) and then tell the biblical story, or tell the biblical story first and then use the script as a way of reinforcing it or as a reflection.

When you are ready to use the script, start by showing the bag and asking some basic questions, such as:

❂ Why do you think my bag is patterned / brown / bright?
❂ What sort of story might be in this bag?
❂ Does it remind you of anything?
❂ What do you think is in my bag?

Once you have done this, move to 'Unpacking the bag'. Choose from the following two approaches: a) is more like a presentation; b) is more interactive. You should keep eye contact with pupils in both approaches.

a) Read the 'Unpacking the bag' verse while the pupils listen. Take the items from the bag one at a time as they are mentioned. Lift them high so that all can see, then place them on the table or carpet in front of you, ready to use.
b) Ask questions as you take items from the bag and ask the pupils to help you unpack.
   ❂ What do you think this is?
   ❂ Have you seen one of these before?
   When pupils have offered their suggestions, read the 'Unpacking the bag' verse, lifting things up as they are mentioned.

> **Tips**
> ✤ Remember to pack the bag in reverse order—with items at the bottom if they are to come out last, and at the top if they are to come out first.
> ✤ Keep small items, such as 'tears', in zipped transparent bags.

Ways of telling the story

The 'cloth' is the storybag® laid flat on the carpet or table. It becomes the arena on which the story is played out. There are suggested actions to use with the scripts, but you can create your own as long as they are appropriate. Whatever actions you use, they should always be unhurried and expressive.

Again, there are two approaches you can use, one more participative than the other:

a) Presentation followed by participation: read the script as a presentation, waiting until the end for pupils' questions and participation.
b) Interactive throughout: ask questions as the story unfolds; encourage children to take part in moving figures and creating sound effects. For example, say, 'I wonder how he feels now?' or 'Could we make wave movements?'

Choose the approach that suits you and adjust the scripts accordingly. Both have their merits: sometimes a presentation without participation can build an atmosphere and have impact, while interaction can make the story feel more 'owned' by the pupils.

You may choose to present the script and do the actions alone, or you may wish to use a helper: one person could read the script while another person does the actions with the bag and items. Alternatively, the script can be recorded beforehand and played while you do the actions.

When you have finished the story script, you might want to choose a few questions from those listed for Key Stages 1 and 2 on page 11, or from the end of the script.

Making their own stories

Pupils can make up their own stories that are not the biblical story (do not use this method with sensitive stories such as the crucifixion). Sometimes this is a good method to use before you present the biblical story. You could say, for example, 'We have a bag, a sun, moon and stars, a deep blue cloth and two people. What story could we make?'

Pupils look at the message of their own stories, then experience a presentation of the biblical story. What is the message of the biblical story? What makes the biblical story different from their story? Interview a Christian about what makes the biblical stories authoritative for them.

Using the scripts with a digital projector

Go to the website **www.barnabasinschools.org.uk/ cooling**. Select the script you want from the menu and follow the instructions. The story can be projected on to a screen with the teacher using the mouse or it can be projected on to an interactive whiteboard.

Pupils can use the interactive website in a number of ways. They can:

- Move the items on the board while the teacher reads the script.
- Use the scripts to retell the story themselves, adding gestures and expression.
- Use the biblical text as a framework to create their own script.
- Create their own stories (see 'Making their own stories', page 9).

Guidance on using the interactive website

1. Some actions cannot be duplicated on a screen or whiteboard, so teachers should still use some physical props, sound effects and gestures. For example, follow instructions in the scripts such as 'point to self', 'throw streamers' and so on.
2. If an item is listed under 'You will need' in the script but is not on the interactive website, assume you will need the physical object (for example, a streamer).
3. Read the script and run through it using the website, adapting as necessary. As your cursor rolls over an item, it will enlarge. For 'Unpacking the bag', just roll the cursor over the items without moving them.
4. Generally, where the script says 'show', 'hold up', 'lift', 'indicate' or 'touch', you can just roll your cursor over the item.
5. Two items cannot be moved at the same time unless they are grouped. For example, the shepherd cannot hold the lost sheep and move. To move two separate characters together, just use small alternating movements of the cursor.

6. Drag and drop the items you want to move, then click on the item you have moved: this will 'set' it in place. Do practise!

In a few scripts, there are special instructions for the web version, as listed below.

- **The battle:** (For younger pupils) Have a paper crown to put on and off your head *as well as* indicating the crown on the interactive website. (For older pupils) Move the crown over the head of the figure on the whiteboard (not on the head), then place it elsewhere on the bag.

- **The footprints:** The people will go in the boat.

- **The seed:** Plants can be placed on top of each other and the seed.

- **The box:** (Both scripts) Use the small square of brown to 'bury' the treasure box.

- **The rocky road:** (For older pupils) You will need a paper heart to tear *as well as* indicating the heart on the interactive website.

- **The whirlwind and the calm:** (Both scripts) Use the patch of blue cloth when the script says 'show blue' or 'flip to the blue side'. (For older pupils) Use a paper weed *as well as* the one on the interactive website.

- **The monster:** (Both scripts) The people will go in the boat. Click on Jesus to make him stand.

- **The beginning:** (Both scripts) Click on the tomb to make it open.

RE thinking skills and follow-up work

A 'thinking skills' approach

The scripts can be used for thinking skills in RE across the age groups. (Pupils might like to use the 'detective badge' idea on page 8 as part of this approach.)

Key Stage 2

After the presentation, use the initial questions to stimulate thinking. Suggested questions are as follows.

⚙ What is interesting about this story?
⚙ What is puzzling or surprising?
⚙ What did you like?
⚙ What did you dislike?
⚙ Does this story have a message or meaning? What is it?

Ask pupils to formulate their own questions about the script (you may want to repeat the presentation, asking pupils to think of the questions they want to ask). They must be questions that concentrate on meaning, ideas and feelings, and cannot be easily answered from the text.

Write up the questions, grouping related questions together (for example, some may all be about right and wrong). Select a question or group of questions to discuss.

Introduce the biblical story that goes with the script as a way of responding to the questions. The biblical story should add to the discussion, not close it down. Explore how the story and the script might interact. Does the biblical story help us to understand the script? Does the script help us to understand the biblical story?

Reflect on what pupils have learned from their discussion. Encourage them to express what they have understood in any form—writing, art, dance and so on.

Key Stage 1

Pupils watch a presentation, after which the teacher creates questions, as follows.

⚙ Questions about feelings: 'Who in the story feels sad? I wonder why that is?'
⚙ Questions about thinking: 'I wonder what the shepherd is thinking?'
⚙ Questions about speech: 'I wonder what the women are saying to each other?'
⚙ Questions about behaviour: 'Why did he stop and help?'
⚙ Questions about meaning: 'What is this story all about?'
⚙ Questions about symbols: 'I wonder why the bag is gold?'

The questions can be asked using the items from the bags, role play and drawings of faces showing different emotions. Wherever possible, reduce abstract questioning.

For more information, go to the site of Robert Fisher, a writer, on whose work this section draws: www.teachingthinking.net.

Follow-up work

The following activities can be used with every script. Select according to the age and aptitude of your pupils and the time you have available. Further suggestions for follow-up work are given in the introduction to each individual script.

Discuss with the pupils the following initial questions:

⚙ The significance of colours, including the colour of the bag.

- Their feelings about the story script. Do different parts of the story make them feel differently? How do characters feel at different moments?
- Who do they think the characters in the script are?
- The meaning of any titles used—for example, 'Man all alone' or 'The one'.
- What do they think is the most important moment in the story and why?
- The meaning of the story script: does it have anything to say to us?

Select from the following activities:

- Pupils can retell the story to themselves, using their own language and the items from the bag. (Make sure everything is safe, replacing items as necessary.) Pupils can make their own bag or box using simple and safe materials.
- Explore the relationship between the text and the story. Use the biblical story to unlock the meaning of the script. Use the script to help children understand the meaning of the biblical story.
- Pupils might like to hear the story again or read a book that is based on the story.
- Does the title help us to understand the story? Can the pupils think of a better title?
- Pupils can express their ideas in art, creating images for part of a story.
- Use a script to develop thinking skills (see page 11).
- Give pupils some new words for feelings. Move the characters about and remind them of how the people felt and why.
- Older pupils might like to write their own script.
- Do they think the author has got it right? Are there places where they would change things?
- Why do they think Christians still read this story?

Plain script

A plain script can be created by photocopying the script and 'whiting out' the actions and the 'Unpacking the bag' verse. Use this as a photocopy master for activities requiring a plain script.

Using the scripts with older pupils

Older pupils might like to try some of the following:

- Use the interactive website.
- Demonstrate the method using a bag and figures, then ask pupils to create their own script and bag for younger pupils, using a plain script and adding their own actions. Shoeboxes covered in giftwrap can replace bags.

- Pupils can create a PowerPoint presentation of the script by using a digital camera, taking photographs of a presentation at key points.
- Create a drama from the script, using pupils rather than figures.
- Pupils can annotate a plain script for reading aloud, preparing it for presentation.
- Turn a script into a book. How will the pupils divide the text? How will they illustrate it?

Creating the storybags®

Fabric bags are simple to make. Alternatively, you can use coloured paper bags. Shoeboxes covered in coloured paper could be used with young children, or you could omit the ribbon on the bags. You would need to adjust the wording of the scripts slightly and add a cloth to the box, in the appropriate colour.

To make a bag, take half a metre of fabric, about 115–122cm in width. Fold the fabric in half, right sides together, and sew down the longer sides (see figure 1).

To make a hem, turn over the top 1cm and iron in place, then turn over another 3cm and iron in place. Machine round the hem, leaving a 2cm gap. Fasten off securely (see figure 2).

Thread 1.5m of ribbon through the hem, entering and leaving by the small gap. Tie the ends of the ribbon to stop them being pulled through (see figure 3).

Turn the bag right-side-out to finish.

> **Note:** You may wish to create a giant Bible storybag® with different images of Bible stories on the front, to show that all the separate stories make one large story (see figure 4).

Finding the objects

The objects suggested in the scripts can be easily found. Many of them will be available in the classroom. Play people or something similar can be used for the characters in the scripts. An easy pattern to make knitted people is provided on page 14. **NB:** All items used *must* be safe for the relevant age group.

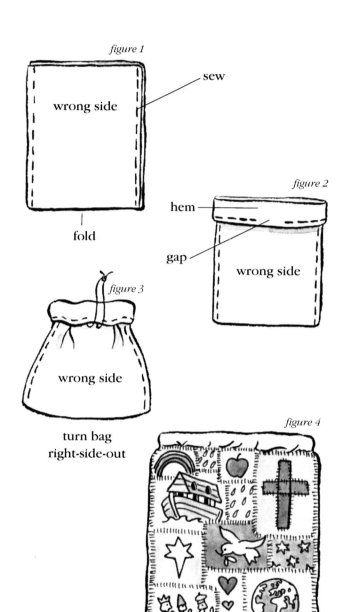

figure 1

sew

wrong side

fold

figure 2

hem

gap

wrong side

figure 3

wrong side

turn bag right-side-out

figure 4

Pattern for knitted people

This is a very basic figure, knitted in stocking stitch (see diagram 1).

Note: Use different body colours to differentiate the figures.

diagram 1

Body

Cast on 26 stitches in body colour.
Knit 1, make one in the next stitch. Repeat to the end of the row. You should have 39 stitches by the end of this first row.
Beginning with a purl row, stocking stitch for 9 rows.
Knit 8 stitches, knit 2 together. Knit 19, knit 2 together. Knit 8.
Knit stocking stitch for 5 rows.
Knit 8 stitches, knit 2 together. Knit 17, knit 2 together. Knit 8.
Knit stocking stitch for 5 rows.
Knit 8 stitches, knit 2 together. Knit 15, knit 2 together. Knit 8.
Knit stocking stitch for 3 rows.
Knit 8 stitches, knit 2 together. Knit 13, knit 2 together. Knit 8.
Knit stocking stitch for 4 rows. Change to face colour.
Purl 2 together to the end of the row.
Stocking stitch for 2 rows.

Knit 2 together. Knit to last 2 stitches. Knit 2 together.
Knit 4, make one in the next 2 stitches. Knit to the last 6 stitches, make one in the next 2 stitches. Knit 4 stitches. Knit stocking stitch for 6 rows.
Knit stocking stitch for the next 3 rows in hair colour. Break the yarn, leaving a long end.
Thread the yarn through remaining stitches and pull up.

Arms

Cast on 12 stitches in body colour.
Knit stocking stitch for 14 rows. Change to face colour. Knit stocking stitch for 4 rows. Break the yarn, leaving a long end.
Thread the yarn through the stitches, pull up, then sew up the seam to create a tube.

Sewing up

Starting at the head, sew up the back seam in the matching colour. Sew down approximately 2.5cm into the body area.

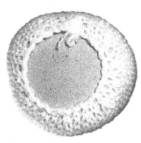

Thread a piece of yarn through the base of the body and pull it until you have a circular opening about 2.5cm in diameter. Sew up the back seam, to approximately 2.5cm from the base. You should now have a tube with a gap in the middle of the seam.

Using a cereal packet, cut three circles of card, 5cm in diameter. Stick the three circles together, one of top of the other, push the card through the gap in the seam and press it down into the base. This will help the figure to stand. Push the stuffing through the gap and into the head and body. This will keep the card in place and stiffen the figure (see diagram 2).

Sew up the back seam using matching yarn. Run a few stitches round, between the head and body, pull and fasten off to create a neck.

Sew up the arms, leaving an opening at the top. Stuff the arms and sew to the sides of the figure.

Using embroidery cotton or wool, embroider two eyes and a mouth if you wish.

Note: a version of this pattern originally appeared in *Firm Foundations Book 2: Exploring Christianity at Foundation Level*, available from www.rmep.co.uk.

The scripts

The coming of the king

The nativity

Using the storybag® in Assembly

To introduce the subject, talk about sending messages. Pupils can role-play sending different types of messages—by courier, by mobile phone (mime), in person, by letter and so on. Send a text message across the room to another member of staff. Discuss the messages that different people might bring. What message might a king bring?

Explain that today's story is about a special king who brought an important message from God. When he grew up, he spread that message through the way he lived and through his teaching. Introduce the Bible story (see Introduction, page 7).

Present the story using the storybag® or the web version (see pages 22–25) and the biblical material (see page 19).

> **Comment**
> Christians believe Jesus was the king that everyone had been waiting for. They believe he brought a message of love and peace that our world still needs to hear.

Reflection

Hold up the ribbons one at a time and ask pupils to reflect:

- ☯ **Silver:** Sometimes we think we are not important, but the angels gave the good news to poor shepherds.
- ☯ **Gold:** The wise men left everything to travel to worship the king. They recognized an important moment.
- ☯ **Brown:** It was hard for Mary and Joseph to obey God. It can be hard for us to obey and do what is right.

Prayer (optional)

Father, we thank you that when we walk through life, whatever road we take, you are there beside us as an invisible friend.

Introduce the subject using some of the material from the assembly introduction (see page 18).

Select the appropriate script and turn to pages 9 and 10 to find ways of using it.

Biblical material

Matthew 1:18—2:18; Luke 1:26–38; 2:1–20

Mary was an ordinary girl from an ordinary town called Nazareth. Today, however, had not been an ordinary day! It had started as usual—she had washed the pots and swept the house—but, as she was busy making bread, suddenly the room was filled with light. Mary covered her eyes and wondered what this could be. 'Don't be afraid,' said the angel. 'I bring you good news: God has chosen you to be the mother of his Son, God's special king, the Messiah.'

Mary thought about this. Every Jewish girl wanted to be chosen for this special job but it was a great responsibility. She thought about Joseph, the man she was about to marry. She thought about her plans for the future—they would have to change! Then she gathered up her courage and said, 'Yes, I will do as God wants.'

Joseph, too, was given a special job by God. His task was to look after Mary and the baby. Together they planned for the birth of this child; this most precious of babies. Long ago, God had promised that a special king would come. For years, people had waited, hoping and dreaming of this king who would bring peace and love.

It was almost time for the baby to be born. Suddenly, all Mary and Joseph's plans were ruined. The emperor, the king of the Romans, told everyone to go back to their home town. Joseph came from Bethlehem, and that was miles away. Mary and Joseph wearily packed their things and started the long journey. The way was difficult and the journey was tiring and, to make matters worse, when they arrived there was nowhere for them to sleep. The town was packed with people.

They went from place to place until finally someone pointed to a stable and said they could sleep there. Joseph did his best to make a bed from the straw, and there in the animals' barn the baby was born. They called him Jesus. Mary wrapped Jesus in a cloth and placed him in the manger—the animals' feed box. No palace for this king!

Meanwhile, in a field near Bethlehem, some shepherds were looking after their sheep, when suddenly they were startled by a bright light. Angels lit up the sky, singing of the birth of a baby king, a king who came with a message of peace and love. Hurriedly the shepherds left their sheep and ran all the way to Bethlehem, where they found the tiny baby, and there they knelt before him.

In a far country, some wise men were gazing at the night sky when they noticed a bright new star. 'This is the sign of a new king,' they said. 'We must go and find this king and offer him our worship.' The wise men packed for a long journey and each added a gift to his bundle. One added gold, another added frankincense and the third added myrrh. Mile after mile they travelled, day after day they followed the star, until finally they came to Bethlehem. There they, too, knelt before the baby king and gave him their gifts.

* The shepherds who had come to the stable went back to their sheep. The wise men who had followed the star returned to their homes. But Mary, Joseph and Jesus could not go home. Herod, the king of that country, had heard of the birth of the baby king and he was angry. *He* was the king and no one else! He would not let another king live. In the quiet of the night, God warned Mary and Joseph to take Jesus and run away to another country where they would be safe. Mary and Joseph obeyed and they took Jesus to Egypt. There they looked after him and kept him safe, but they were far from their family and friends. They were strangers in a strange land.

* Can be omitted

Note: For a comment on this story, see the assembly section (page 18).

Follow-up activities

(See also pages 11 and 12.) Select from these activities according to the age and aptitude of your pupils.

1. Create a display by covering a board with deep blue paper and adding two-dimensional versions of the items from the bag. Add questions and comments from the pupils. Sections of the script could act as captions. Explore with pupils how life can be like a road. Pupils can draw their own 'life road' and decide on a colour for it.

2. Create a Christmas card reflecting the ideas or symbols in this script and the biblical story—for example, a baby king, life as a road. What would you write inside? Alternatively, work with the children to create their own nativity play based on the script, that will communicate its message.

3. Encourage pupils to listen to music as they reflect on the story. They can express their own ideas and understanding through sound or music. Some suggested pieces are as follows.

- CDs of carols and Christmas music from different cultures (available from Aid agencies and Christian bookshops)
- 'Unto us a child is born' from *Messiah* by Handel
- *Christmas Oratorio* by Bach

4. In Script 2, Jesus is born where 'hopes, dreams and promises meet'. What do you think these 'hopes, dreams and promises' were? Explore some biblical prophecies: Isaiah 9:2; 11:1–9; Micah 4:1–4. Write them on scrolls and add them to the display. What hopes and dreams for a better world do people have today?

5. Use the technique called 'Time, place, weather and person'.

- In one corner of an A4 sheet, choose a time and write it down, or draw a clock.
- Choose a person from the story and draw them in another corner.
- In the third corner, draw a place where that person could be at your chosen time.
- Finally, decide on the weather and draw a weather symbol in the remaining corner.

For example, you might end up with midnight, Mary, in the stable, cold and damp. Write a poem or piece of prose from that person's point of view in that situation.

6. Explore how artists express their understanding of this story, and encourage pupils to do the same. Useful websites may include:

- www.Jesusmafa.com > mini posters
- www.nationalgallery.org.uk > search 'nativity'
- www.mccrimmons.com > posters > seasonal > Christmas
- www.biblical-art.com > biblical subject > New Testament > Gospels, Jesus: nativity and childhood > nativity
- www.biblepicturegallery.com
- www.heqigallery.com (browse galleries)

Christmas images, activities and lesson plans can be found on the CD *Cracking Christmas*. Multicultural Christmas images can also be found in the pack *Born Among Us* (The Methodist Church/USPG/CMS). Both are available from www.stapleford-centre.org.

Symbols used in this story

- Blue: the blue planet (earth).
- The roads: a journey through life.
- Stars and angels: guidance and messages from God.
- The meeting place: where things came together (hints of fulfilment of prophecy).
- Angels: messengers from heaven.
- Gold: heaven, glory and celebration.
- The voice: God.
- Beginning and end: birth and death, the end of one era and the start of another.

Note: many nativity pictures carry a hint of the crucifixion to come. For example, in the *Mystic Nativity* by Botticelli (National Gallery), the ass has a cross in dark fur on its back.

Reflective activity

Cover a table with an attractive cloth and lay out the storybag®. Add the angels' message: 'Peace on earth, goodwill to all people'. Place a question asking pupils to reflect on how they can bring peace and love at home and school. Add a basket containing pieces of coloured paper, pencils and mini Christmas crackers (with the bang and contents removed).

Pupils write, draw or dictate their suggestion and insert it in a cracker, close the cracker, add their name and keep it somewhere safe. The crackers can be opened at the end of term, but pupils only read their own suggestion unless they want to share ideas.

('Live' crackers must be pulled with adult supervision.)

Assessment

Assess the pupils' understanding by observing them replaying the script, or ask them to talk or write about the display.

Background information and understanding the story

Christians believe that Jesus is God's Son, who came to earth to bring God's message of peace and love and to bring people into a never-ending relationship with God by rescuing them from wrong. These themes link Christmas and Easter together. Jesus lived his message and never tried to force people to accept it; that is why there is still war and wrong things in the world.

One of the titles Jesus is given is 'Immanuel', which means 'God with us'. Christians believe that Jesus experienced human life, so he knows and understands what it is like.

Various prophets spoke of the Messiah who would come ('Messiah' means 'the anointed one'). The Messiah was a special king sent from God. Kings were anointed with oil in biblical times. Christians believe that Jesus was the Messiah foretold by the prophets.

The Bible says that the baby Jesus was laid in a manger, which was an animals' feeding trough. It is not unreasonable to deduce that the manger was in a stable, although there is no mention of a stable in the biblical story. Alternatively, the manger could have been in the animals' section of a poor person's house. Animals were often kept in the lower part of homes rather than in separate stables.

The wise men came from the area known today as Iran and Iraq. The gifts they brought have been interpreted symbolically as gold for a king, myrrh for suffering (it was used in pain relief) and frankincense for a priest (it was used in worship).

The shepherds were probably hired shepherds who lived out on the hills. They were of the lowest strata in society, so both rich and poor people are present in this story.

Useful websites

The websites listed below are active at the time of writing.

- ✪ www.topmarks.co.uk > search 'Christmas'
- ✪ www.request.org.uk > infants > festivals > Christmas
- ✪ www.refuel.org.uk
- ✪ www.textweek.com/art/art.htm > Jacob to Mustard Seed > Jesus/Christ > Birth of Jesus *or* Nativity

You will need:

❖ A dark blue storybag
❖ Small paper stars
❖ One large star
❖ 10 'people':
  3 wise men,
  3 shepherds,
  1 angel, 1 man,
  1 woman, 1 baby
❖ Sheep

Questions
(See also page 11.)

❂ Who are the people in this story?
❂ Who is the baby?
❂ Why did he bring a message of peace and love? *(See Luke 2:14; John 3:16)*

Script 1

Unpacking the bag

*My bag is blue, the colour of our world: the blue planet.
There are stars in my bag that pepper the sky,
and one large star that points the way.
There is an angel in my bag with a message about a king.
There are men in my bag who watch stars,
and others who watch sheep.
There are a man and a woman in my bag who care for a baby
who comes with a message of peace and love.*

The story

Our story takes place on a deep blue cloth *(show bag)* for it starts on an evening when the deep blue sky is darkening into night *(put bag down, and smooth)*. A man and woman go from place to place, looking for a room *(lift and place man and woman)*. They are tired, they are weary. They have walked a long, long way and the woman is about to have a baby *(walk man and woman)*. They keep knocking on doors, hoping someone will give them a room for the night *(knock, shake head)*. Every house is full *(move figures, knock and shake head)*. All the inns are crowded *(move figures, knock and shake head)*. There is no room for them *(move figures, knock and shake head)*. In the end they find a stable and there the baby is born *(place baby with man and woman)*—a baby king, born in a stable.

Our story takes place on a deep blue cloth *(indicate bag)* because, on a hillside far away, some shepherds sit under the deep blue sky, looking after their sheep *(place shepherds and sheep)*. Suddenly, they hear angels telling them a new king has been born *(place angel near shepherds)*. Leaving their sheep, they go in search of the king *(move shepherds towards baby)*. They find the baby king and worship him *(place shepherds close to baby)*.

Our story takes place on a deep blue cloth *(indicate bag)* because, far away, men are looking at the midnight sky that is dotted with stars *(place three wise men and scatter small stars)*. Suddenly, they notice a new star—a great star that tells them a special king has been born *(place large star)*. Quickly they pack their bags and follow the star; travelling for miles, travelling for days, always going where the star leads *(move men and star around)*. The men who follow the star find their way to the baby king and they, too, worship and bring him gifts *(place men and star near baby)*. Everyone knows they have seen something amazing, the birth of a king who comes with a message of peace and love.

Reproduced with permission from *Bible Storybags®* published by BRF 2011 (978 0 85746 073 8) www.barnabasinschools.org.uk

Script 2

Unpacking the bag

My bag is blue, the colour of our world: the blue planet.
There are three roads in my bag:
the first road is the colour of starlight;
the second road is the colour of angels' wings;
the third road is the colour of the earth itself.
There are stars in my bag that pepper the sky,
and one large star that points the way.
There is an angel in my bag with a message from heaven.
There are men in my bag who watch stars.
There are shepherds in my bag who watch sheep.
There are a man and a woman who tread the hard road of obedience.
There is a baby, born into a world he came to change.

> **Note:** For layout, see picture 'The coming of the king' on inside back cover.

You will need:
- A dark blue storybag
- Small paper stars
- One large star
- 10 'people':
  3 wise men,
  3 shepherds,
  1 angel, 1 man,
  1 woman, 1 baby
- Sheep
- A gold ribbon
- A silver ribbon
- A longer brown ribbon

The story

Our story takes place on a blue cloth, the colour of our world.	*Place bag*
It starts with three roads… a star-lit road…	*Place gold ribbon*
an angel-lit road…	*Place silver ribbon*
a hard road.	*Place brown ribbon*
This is the story of three roads, but one journey…	*Hold up three fingers, then fold down two*
a journey to a beginning that is also an end.	
In a land far away…	*Place three men near gold road*
three men gaze at the stars in the midnight sky. Stars stud the darkness…	*Scatter stars around them*

Reproduced with permission from *Bible Storybags*® published by BRF 2011 (978 0 85746 073 8) www.barnabasinschools.org.uk

but one star shines brighter
than them all...
and calls to them.   *Place large star above gold road*

It calls them to leave their homes...
and follow a star-lit road to a king.   *Place men on gold road*

It calls them to a journey to a beginning,
that is also an end.

On a hillside in the country...   *Place shepherds near silver road*

shepherds listen to the silence
of the midnight sky.
Suddenly, the silence is split by
the songs of angels.   *Place angel near shepherds*

One angel sings louder than them all,
calling the shepherds to leave
their sheep...   *Place shepherds on silver road*

and follow an angel-lit road to a king.
It calls them to a journey to a beginning,
that is also an end.

In a small town...   *Place man and woman at
                                                                      far end of the brown road*

a man and a woman wearily pack their bags.
As they look at the midnight sky,
no star calls to them.   *Lift and replace star*

As they listen to the midnight silence,
no angels sing.   *Lift and replace angel*

The sky remains dark and silent.
Before them stretches a hard road.   *Indicate road*

It calls them to leave their home...   *Move man and woman
                                                                   close to the meeting point*

it calls them to travel on a way
unlit by stars and angels.
It calls them to a beginning,
that is also an end.

Reproduced with permission from *Bible Storybags®* published by BRF 2011 (978 0 85746 073 8) www.barnabasinschools.org.uk

THE COMING OF THE KING (THE NATIVITY)

At a stable three roads meet…	*Touch meeting point*
a star-lit road…	*Lift and replace star*
an angel-lit road…	*Lift and replace angel*
a hard road.	*Touch brown road*
This is the place where hopes, dreams and promises meet.	*Place baby where roads meet*
At the meeting place a baby is born…	

born on the earth,
born into the world he came to change.

Above the place a star shines…	*Place large star near baby*
In the heavens the angels sing…	*Move angel near baby*
And people who had travelled other roads come to worship.	*Move shepherds and wise men near the baby*
But a voice calls to the family to leave this place, for it is dangerous.	*Indicate family*
The man and woman know they must begin another journey. They look at the three roads…	*Indicate each road in turn*
the star-lit road… the angel-lit road… the hard road. They step on to the hard road, the road where the voice calls.	*Move family to the end of the brown road*

It is calling them to a journey to an end,
that is also a beginning.

THE COMING OF THE KING (THE NATIVITY)

Questions
(See also page 11.)

- Who is the baby?
- Whose voice is calling?
- What are the three roads?
- Can a beginning be an end? Can an end be a beginning?
- Can a baby change the world? Did this baby change the world?

The voice

John the Baptist and Jesus' baptism

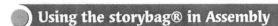

Using the storybag® in Assembly

To introduce the subject, talk about times when we do things wrong and we need to say sorry and start again. Using a felt-tip pen, write some things people say sorry for on laminated sheets of card—for example, lying, stealing, or hurting friends. The bad feeling we sometimes get when we do, say or think things that are wrong is called 'guilt'. Forgiveness is like someone wiping out the wrongs. It removes the guilt and gives a fresh start.

Ask pupils to wipe out the wrongs by washing the cards with water and a cloth. Do stress that forgiveness is not allowing the wrong to continue! Explain that today's story is all about being sorry and being forgiven. Introduce the Bible story (see Introduction, page 7).

> **Note:** This story covers John the Baptist and Jesus' baptism. You may wish to use only one section of the story.

Present the story using the storybag® or the web version (see pages 29–31) and the biblical material (see page 27).

> **Comment**
> Christians believe that God always forgives, but forgiveness is about being sorry and being willing to change, not just about being sorry.

Reflection

Pour some water into a bowl and ask pupils to listen to the sound. As they listen, suggest that they might like to think of times when they have said sorry and been forgiven.

Prayer *(optional)*

Father God, we thank you that there is always forgiveness and there is nothing that can separate someone from your love.

Using the storybag® in RE

Introduce the subject using some of the material from the assembly introduction (see page 26).

Select the appropriate script and turn to pages 9 and 10 to find ways of using it.

Biblical material

Mark 1:1–11; Matthew 3:13–17; Luke 3:1–22

The wilderness is a quiet place—a desert of rock and earth; blazing heat by day, freezing cold by night. The wilderness is a wild place—few sounds are heard; only the call of animals and the cry of birds break the silence.

It was unusual to hear a human voice in the wilderness, but that is what happened. In the desert a man appeared who began to talk of God. The man who spoke was called John. He lived on the edge of the desert, surviving on what he could find. People travelled to the desert to hear John, for John spoke about being sorry and changing. He spoke of greedy people becoming generous; he spoke of people who told lies becoming truthful. He spoke of a fresh start. He spoke of losing guilt and finding forgiveness.

John stepped into the river and invited others in. He told people that being baptized (dipping under the water and coming up again) was like a picture of God's forgiveness. Just as the water washed people's bodies clean, so forgiveness could wash their lives clean. They could start again.

John told people to get ready, for there was someone much greater than him coming—someone with great power. One day Jesus came to the river and John pointed him out to the people, saying that this was the Powerful One. Jesus waded into the river but John refused to baptize him. 'You have done no wrong,' said John. 'You don't need to be baptized!' But Jesus asked John to baptize him anyway, to show others that this was the right thing to do. As Jesus came up from the water, a dove spiralled from the sky and there was a sound like thunder. A different voice was heard saying, 'This is my beloved Son. Listen to him.'

Note: For a comment on this story, see the assembly section (page 26).

Follow-up activities

(See also pages 11 and 12.) Select from these activities according to the age and aptitude of your pupils.

1. Encourage pupils to reflect on the story as they listen to music. They can express their own ideas and understanding through sound and music. Some suggested pieces are as follows.

- *Sinfonia Antarctica* by Ralph Vaughan Williams
- 'Under the stars' from *The Lion King* by H. Zimmer
- 'Frozen oceans' from *The Blue Planet* by G. Fenton (BBC soundtrack)

2. Pupils can express their own understanding of the story using dance and drama. Create a water dance using fabrics or streamers. How could they express water symbolically washing away wrong?

3. Create a display by covering a board with light brown paper or hessian and adding two-dimensional versions of the items from the bag, using various art techniques. Add questions and comments from the pupils. Sections of the script could act as captions. Older pupils can add an explanation of water as a symbol of cleansing.

4. Explore how artists express their understanding of this story, and encourage pupils to do the same. The websites listed below are active at the time of writing.

- www.Jesusmafa.com > mini posters
- www.nationalgallery.org.uk > search 'baptism of Christ'
- www.biblical-art.com > biblical subject > New Testament > Gospels, John the Baptist *and* Gospels, Jesus, Public Ministry: Preparations
- www.biblepicturegallery.com

5. Explore the religious words used in this script ('holy', 'sorry' and so on). What do they mean? Why are they there? Stretch and shape key words (either drawing them freehand or using a software package) so that they flow like water across the page. Explore the message of John the Baptist. Does his message apply today? Look up his teaching and create a short presentation on him (see Luke 3:1–16).

6. Create a kenning for John the Baptist that will capture his role and life. A kenning describes things without naming them. For example, 'word scribbler' would be a kenning for a pen. 'World maker' might be a kenning for God. If you would like to, read the poem 'John, John the Baptist' by Charles Causley from *Whispering in God's Ear* (ed. Alan MacDonald, LionHudson plc, 1994).

Symbols used in this story

- ✪ River: going under the water and up again symbolizes the death of an old life and the beginning of a new one.
- ✪ Water: cleansing people from sin.
- ✪ The wilderness or desert: a place for people to meet God (see page 34).
- ✪ Dove: God's Holy Spirit (God unseen and everywhere; God in action in the world).

Reflective activity

Display the storybag® on a table with an attractive cloth. Make available some appropriate children's wet-wipes and a child-safe face-paint crayon. Pupils can, if they wish, make a mark on their hand and remove it with a wet-wipe as a reminder of the 'washing' in the story that symbolized forgiveness.

Assessment

Assess the pupils' understanding by observing them replaying the script, or ask them to talk about the display or write about it.

Background information and understanding the story

There had been no prophets in Israel for 400 years, and then John the Baptist appeared, looking and sounding like a prophet. His message was to get ready for the Messiah, the special king sent by God. This meant getting ready on the inside—being as pure as possible. John's teaching attracted large numbers but his popularity began to worry the authorities.

John baptized people in the river Jordan, which was a dangerous place (wild animals lived there).

Christians believe that Jesus came to be baptized in order to set an example and also to identify with humankind.

Christians believe that Jesus was the promised Messiah, God's Son, who experienced human life.

Baptism was an outward symbol of wanting to be clean 'on the inside' in attitudes, feeling, thinking and behaviour. It was about losing guilt and regret and finding forgiveness and a new start.

The voice of God is *Bat Kol* in Hebrew, which means literally 'The daughter of a voice'.

Useful websites

The websites listed below are active at the time of writing.

- ✪ www.theway2go.org > the hub > light blue ball > life's big moments
- ✪ www.educhurch.org.uk > themes > events > baptism
- ✪ www.request.org.uk (browse teacher's area)
- ✪ www.textweek.com/art/art.htm > Jacob to Mustard Seed > John the Baptist *and* Baptism of Jesus

Script 1

Unpacking the bag

My bag is brown, the colour of earth baked by the sun.
There is a river in my bag, cool and clean.
There are people in my bag who go to the river,
and a man who speaks to them.
There is someone in my bag who comes to bring forgiveness.

The story

Our story starts on a rough brown cloth *(hold up bag)*, for it starts in a wild place where few people live *(put bag down, and smooth)*. Through the wild place runs a river *(place ribbon)*. A man lives there *(place John on bag)*. People gather there to hear him speak about God *(place crowd on bag)*. He speaks *(lift John)* of losing and finding—losing guilt and finding forgiveness. He speaks of a fresh start *(place John in river)*. The people listen and follow him into the river and out again *(move crowd through river and out)*. They feel the water washing their skin *(run your hand up your arm*)* and they feel the forgiveness taking away their guilt *(touch heart)*.

The man *(lift John)* tells them of someone who will come to bring love and forgiveness *(replace John)*. Someone comes *(place Jesus on bag)* and he goes into the river *(place Jesus in river)*. He does not go to lose his guilt *(shake head)*, for he has done nothing wrong. He does not go to find forgiveness *(shake head)*, for he is good. He goes to show the way. When he comes up from the water *(move Jesus out of river)*, a voice is heard saying, 'This is my Son, my beloved Son. Listen to him.'

* If you wish, you can use water in a bottle poured out into a bowl. Adjust text as necessary.

You will need:
- ❖ A rough light brown bag (hessian if possible)
- ❖ A shiny blue ribbon for the river
- ❖ 6 people: 4 crowd members, 1 John the Baptist, 1 Jesus

Questions
(See also page 11.)

- ❂ Who is the 'voice'?
- ❂ Who is the 'someone'?
- ❂ What do people lose and find?

Reproduced with permission from *Bible Storybags®* published by BRF 2011 (978 0 85746 073 8) www.barnabasinschools.org.uk

THE VOICE (JOHN THE BAPTIST AND JESUS' BAPTISM)

Script 2

You will need:
- ❖ A rough light brown bag (hessian if possible)
- ❖ A shiny blue ribbon for the river
- ❖ 6 people: 4 crowd members, 1 John the Baptist, 1 Jesus
- ❖ A paper dove
- ❖ Coloured pieces of paper with key words written on them (Sorry, change, help, holy, forgive, get ready)

Unpacking the bag

My bag is brown, the brown of earth baked by the sun.
There is a river in my bag, cool and clear.
There are people who want to lose guilt and find forgiveness.
There is a man in my bag who lives in a wild place.
There is someone in my bag who comes to lead the way.
There is a dove in my bag that spirals to earth.
There are words in my bag that are important.

The story

Our story takes place on a rough brown cloth.	*Place bag and smooth it*
It starts in a wild place, far from the safety of home. Through the wild place runs a river…	*Place river*
deep and cold. It is a place of losing and finding.	
This is the story of a voice…	*Place John on one side of river*
crying in the wild place. The voice cries, 'Change'…	*Place the words around him*
The voice cries, 'Get ready'… The voice cries, 'Holy.'	
Men and women listen to the voice.	*Place men and women on other side of river*
Their voices whisper, 'Sorry'…	*Add words around them*
Their voices cry, 'Forgive us'… Their voices pray, 'Help us to live holy.'	

Reproduced with permission from *Bible Storybags*® published by BRF 2011 (978 0 85746 073 8) www.barnabasinschools.org.uk

THE VOICE (JOHN THE BAPTIST AND JESUS' BAPTISM)

John wades into the river…	*Place John in river*
and men and women follow.	*People pass through river and to the far side of the cloth*

In its waters they lose their guilt and fear…
In its waters they find forgiveness.

Then he comes, the one they were waiting for, the one they were getting ready for.	*Place Jesus on cloth*
He does not enter the river to lose his guilt…	*Place Jesus in river*
for he has none. He does not go into its waters to find forgiveness…	*Shake head*
for he has done no wrong. He goes into the waters to lead the way.	*Walk John and Jesus out of river*
Rising from the waters, the heavens crack…	*Spiral dove*

and a dove-descending Spirit spirals
to the earth.
Then another voice is heard…
a daughter of a voice crying,
'This is my beloved, my beloved Son'.

Questions
(See also page 11.)

- Who is the one they were waiting for?
- What voices are heard? What could 'daughter of a voice' mean?
- Why do people go into the river?
- What do they lose and find?
- People say, 'Help us to live holy.' Holy what?

Reproduced with permission from *Bible Storybags®* published by BRF 2011 (978 0 85746 073 8) www.barnabasinschools.org.uk

THE VOICE (JOHN THE BAPTIST AND JESUS' BAPTISM)

The battle

Jesus is tempted

●●●

Using the storybag® in Assembly

To introduce the subject, talk about times when we are faced with temptations. Use role-play where appropriate, showing different things we might be tempted to do, such as taking something that belongs to someone else. Talk about how we are tempted and how it can be like a battle inside—a battle with ourselves.

Invite a pupil to act as the person being tempted, and place pupils either side of him or her, holding speech bubbles that represent the good and bad thoughts going through their mind. Explain that today's story is all about temptations. It is a story about someone who had some big decisions to make and was tempted to make the wrong ones. Introduce the Bible story (see Introduction, page 7).

> Take it, no one will know!

> No, it's wrong.

Present the story using the storybag® or the web version (see pages 35–37) and the biblical material (see page 33).

Comment

Christians believe that Jesus understands what it is like to be tempted. Jesus had to make a decision about how he used his power (the battle between self and service). Should his power be used for personal benefit or for serving others? He was tempted to use his power wrongly, but he resisted. Christians also believe that God can help them to resist wrong.

Reflection

Ask pupils to trace the word 'NO' on their hands using one finger. While they do this, they can think about a time when they said 'No' to temptation.

Prayer (optional)

Heavenly Father, we thank you that we do not have to struggle against temptation by ourselves, but that we can ask the Holy Spirit for help.

Using the storybag® in RE

Introduce the subject using some of the material from the assembly introduction (see page 32).

Select the appropriate script and turn to pages 9 and 10 to find ways of using it.

Biblical material

Luke 4:1–13
See also Matthew 7:13–14 (CEV):

Go in through the narrow gate. The gate to destruction is wide, and the road that leads there is easy to follow. A lot of people go through that gate. But the gate to life is very narrow. The road that leads there is so hard to follow that only a few people find it.

> **Note:** Avoid using the Good News Bible for this passage, as it translates 'destruction' as 'hell'.

After Jesus was baptized, he went into the wilderness, and there he spent time thinking and praying. During that time, he went without food. It was time for him to start his work, but first there were some big decisions to make. Jesus knew he had great power and was a special king—the Messiah—but how should he use his power? What sort of king should he be?

In the quiet of the wilderness, Jesus struggled with temptation. He was tempted to use his power for himself, but he thought about what it said in the Bible and he said, 'No'. He was tempted to use his power to do stunts to impress people and make them follow him. It would be quick and easy and make him famous. But again he thought about what it said in the Bible and he said, 'No'. He was tempted to gain even more power by serving evil. Once more he thought about what it said in the Bible and once more he said, 'No'.

Jesus made the decision to use his power to serve others. He would be a servant-king. He left the wilderness and started his work, but he knew there would be other times when he would be tempted to take the easy but wrong way.

> **Note:** For a comment on this story, see the assembly section (page 32).

Follow-up activities

(See also pages 11 and 12.) Select from these activities according to the age and aptitude of your pupils.

1. Encourage pupils to listen to music as they reflect on the story. They can express their own ideas and understanding through sound or music. Some suggested pieces are as follows.

- All music suggestions on page 27
- Opening of 'Saturn' from *The Planets* by Gustav Holst

2. Create a display by covering a board with light brown paper and adding two-dimensional versions of the items from the bag, using various art techniques. Add questions and comments from the pupils. Sections of the script could act as captions. At the fork, add some of the temptations or difficult decisions that people face today.

3. Pupils can create a dance to express their own ideas concerning temptation. For example, they could use movements to express being pulled in two directions.

4. Discuss the 'wilderness' times that we all go through. Draw a wilderness and write on the rocks and sand the difficult decisions and temptations that people face in life.

5. What 'weapons' do people use in the 'battle' with temptation? Write some of them on weapon-shaped pieces of paper. Older pupils might like to work out strategies for resisting temptation and produce some advice guides.

6. Explore how artists express their understanding of this story, and encourage pupils to do the same. The websites listed below are active at the time of writing.

- www.biblical-art.com > biblical subject > New Testament > Gospels, Jesus, public ministry: preparations
- www.abcgallery.com > search > I. Kramskoy
- www.biblepicturegallery.com
- www.Jesusmafa.com > mini posters

Images of wildernesses can be found on sites such as www.worldbiomes.com.

Symbols used in this story

☺ The wilderness: a metaphor for the difficult times in life.
☺ The road or path: life's journey, which can be hard or easy. A fork symbolizes a choice.
☺ The broad path: the easy path through life.
☺ The narrow path: the difficult path through life—trying to stand up for what is right.
☺ Weapons: the means used to defeat temptation.
☺ Battle: the struggle between good and evil; temptation.
☺ Mirror: facing yourself; internal battle.

Reflective activity

Cover a table with hessian and display the bag and items. Have pictures of wildernesses displayed, and add a foil tray of play sand. Place relevant questions to think about around the area. These can vary according to the type of school: for example, 'What do you do when you have a difficult decision to make?' or 'In what ways is temptation like a battle?'

Invite children, if they wish, to spend a few moments in the reflective area. They can draw the road and the fork in the sand with their finger and think about times when they have faced temptation or a difficult decision.

Assessment

Assess the pupils' understanding by observing them replaying the script, or ask them to talk about the display or write about it.

Background information and understanding the story

The temptations came at the beginning of Jesus' ministry, when he had to decide what sort of Messiah (king) he would be. He chose the way of suffering and service rather than power and popularity for himself.

Jesus resisted the temptation to:

☺ Use his power for himself.
☺ Use his power to gain quick popularity and stun people into believing in him.
☺ Gain power by serving evil.

The wilderness was traditionally the place where people met God. God had led the Israelites through the wilderness when they escaped from slavery in Egypt. The Ten Commandments were given in the wilderness, and Elijah met God in the wilderness.

Jesus was in the wilderness for 40 days and 40 nights. This reflects the 40 years that the Israelites were in the wilderness after leaving Egypt.

Useful websites

The websites listed below are active at the time of writing.

☺ www.textweek.com/art/art.htm > Jacob to Mustard Seed > Jesus/Christ > Temptation
☺ www.biblicalplaces.com > search 'Judean wilderness'

Script 1

Unpacking the bag

My bag is brown, the colour of dry earth.
There is a road in my bag that cuts through the wilderness.
There is a man who is all alone in my bag.
There is a crown in my bag, a crown for a king.

The story

This is the wilderness, the place where no one lives *(put bag down and smooth)*. This is the road that goes through the wilderness *(place road)*. This is the man who is all alone *(place Jesus at beginning of road)*. He walks the road into the wilderness. He has come to the wilderness to be alone *(move him along road a little)*. He wants time to think *(indicate your head)*. He wants time to pray *(lace fingers together to indicate prayer)*.

The man who is all alone *(lift and replace figure)* thinks about the job he has to do, and in the quiet of the wilderness no one disturbs him *(shake head, then place finger on lips: 'shhhhh')*. The man thinks about what he should do *(indicate your head)*. 'I am a king,' he thinks *(hold up crown)*. 'But what sort of king shall I be?' *(place crown on bag)*.

(Place crown on your head) 'I could use my power to get things for myself; that would make life easy' *(place crown on bag)*. 'But it would not be right' *(shake head)*.

(Place crown on your head) 'I could use my power to make people follow me; that would be exciting' *(place crown on bag)*. 'But it would not be right' *(shake head)*.

(Place crown on your head) 'I could get everyone to bow down to me and I would feel really important' *(place crown on bag)*. 'But it would not be right' *(shake head)*.

(Place crown on your head) 'I could be a loving king who helps others; that would be hard, but that would be right' *(nod)*.

The man who is all alone prays *(lace fingers together in prayer)* and he decides to be a king who serves others. He has made his decision; he leaves the wilderness *(walk him down the road and off the bag)*; he goes out into the world to be a servant king *(remove crown)*.

You will need:

* A bag made from desert camouflage material
* 1 person (Jesus)
* A brown ribbon
* Adult-size gold crown (circlet of gold card)

Questions
(See also page 11.)

* Who is the man who is all alone?
* What decision does he make?
* Why does he go to the wilderness to pray and think?

Reproduced with permission from *Bible Storybags®* published by BRF 2011 (978 0 85746 073 8) www.barnabasinschools.org.uk

Script 2

You will need:

❖ A bag made from desert camouflage material
❖ 1 person (Jesus)
❖ A brown ribbon
❖ Adult-size gold crown (circlet of gold card)
❖ A piece of mirror card
❖ A thin, short strip of brown ribbon to add to the road (see picture three on inside cover)

Note: A version of this script originally appeared in *REthinking Book 9: God, Faith and the Classroom*, available from www.stapleford-centre.org.

Unpacking the bag

My bag is brown, the colour of dry earth.
There is a road in my bag, a road of decisions.
There is a man in my bag who is all alone.
There is a mirror in my bag in which we see ourselves.

The story

This is the wilderness…	*Place bag*
and the wilderness is a wild place…	*Smooth bag*
a place of battle… a place where you face yourself…	*Place mirror*
This is the road that winds through the wilderness.	*Place road*
A man who is all alone walks on the road…	*Place Jesus at the beginning of the road*
through the wilderness…	*Run finger along road*
deep into the wild place. He carries his weapons within himself…	*Point to self*
as he comes to the battle.	*Show mirror*
In the heart of the wilderness the road forks.	*Add fork (thin strip of ribbon)*
Two paths lie ahead: a broad path, easy and smooth…	*Indicate with hands wide*
a narrow path, hard and rough.	*Indicate with hands narrowed*
It is here, where the roads fork, that the battle will be fought.	*Touch fork*

Reproduced with permission from *Bible Storybags®* published by BRF 2011 (978 0 85746 073 8) www.barnabasinschools.org.uk

THE BATTLE (JESUS IS TEMPTED)

It is here that choices will be made.
This is the place of decisions.

At the fork in the road the battle begins...	*Move Jesus to fork*
the battle between self and service...	*Point to self, then others*
the battle to decide what sort of king he should be...	*Place crown*

For the man who is all alone is a king.

The battle is fierce and long...	*Lift mirror*

but in the wilderness there is a victory.
The king has made his decision.

The man who is all alone continues his walk through the wilderness...	*Place Jesus on narrow road*
and out into the world. He takes the narrow path...	*Walk him down road and off the bag*
still carrying his weapons within himself...	*Point to self*

for the battle is not over, only paused.

At times we walk in our own wilderness.	*Circle wilderness with finger*
We fight our battles at the point where the road forks...	*Indicate fork*
the place of decisions. It is the place where we choose between self and service...	*Point to self, then others*
We each choose the road by which we leave the wilderness and go out into the world...	*Indicate roads*
the broad and easy way or...	*Hands apart*
the narrow but hard way.	*Hands closer together*

Questions
(See also page 11.)

- Who is the man who is all alone?
- What was the battle and who is the battle with?
- Why is there a mirror in this story?
- What are the weapons?
- What do the paths and the fork represent?

Reproduced with permission from *Bible Storybags®* published by BRF 2011 (978 0 85746 073 8) www.barnabasinschools.org.uk

THE BATTLE (JESUS IS TEMPTED)

The footprints

Jesus chooses his first disciples

● ●

Using the storybag® in Assembly

To introduce the subject, play 'Follow my leader'. You can do this with a small group of pupils to demonstrate. Talk about followers and following. Football teams have followers. What other type of followers might there be? Today's story is about people who followed a teacher. Introduce the Bible story (see Introduction, page 7).

Present the story using the storybag® or the web version (see pages 41–43) and the biblical material (see page 39).

Comment

This is a story about the disciples following Jesus. Christians believe that Jesus still invites people to follow him. The invitation is often silent or comes via other people. It does not always mean leaving jobs and homes. Usually (but not always) people make the decision to serve God wherever they are when they become a Christian.

Reflection

Create a short PowerPoint presentation of different people that others follow. As you show the images, ask pupils to think about people who set an example that it is right to follow and people we should not follow.

Prayer *(optional)*

Heavenly Father, we all follow different people in life. Sometimes we follow people who set a good example; sometimes we follow people who set a bad example. Help us to follow those who lead in the right way.

Introduce the subject using some of the material from the assembly introduction (see page 38).

Select the appropriate script and turn to pages 9 and 10 to find ways of using it.

> **Note:** Stress that the disciples were adults and Simon and Andrew already knew and trusted Jesus (John 1:35). They were not going off with a stranger.

Biblical material

Matthew 4:18–22; Mark 1:16–20; Luke 5:1–11 (see also Matthew 9:9–13; 10:1–4; John 1:35–50)

One day, Jesus was walking by the Sea of Galilee (which is really a lake) when he saw two brothers fishing. Their names were Andrew and Simon. 'Follow me,' said Jesus. The men put down their nets and followed. A little further along the lake they came to another boat, and in the boat were two brothers called James and John. Once again Jesus said, 'Follow me', and the two fishermen left their nets and followed. Jesus invited these fishermen to do a different sort of work. He called them to bring people into God's love, rather than bringing fish into a net.

> **Note:** For a comment on this story, see the assembly section (page 38).

Follow-up activities

(See also pages 11 and 12.) Select from these activities according to the age and aptitude of your pupils.

1. Make footprint shapes by drawing round feet. On the foot shapes write some of the teachings of the teacher (Jesus). Some of the following references may be helpful (select according to the age of your pupils):

John 15:12
Luke 6:31
Matthew 6:19–21
Matthew 6:25–34

2. The disciples were learners—people who listened to Jesus' teaching in order to put it into practice in the way that they lived. Discuss some of the teachings. How easy or difficult are they to put into practice? Role-play situations where these teachings might be relevant. Create short dramas to illustrate each one.

3. Create a display using a sandy coloured background with a border made of foot shapes. Add a blue area for the water and staple two cardboard boat shapes to the display, leaving the tops open. Slot people into the boats and add nets and fish. Add the Jesus figure on the sand. Add questions and comments from the pupils. Sections of the script could act as captions.

4. Encourage pupils to respond to the story using mime or dance. Concentrate on following, leading, walking, stopping, beckoning and so on.

5. Create an act of worship based on this story that your class could lead. Things to think about might be:

- How you will present the story.
- Drama, dance and music you could use.
- Prayers or reflections.

6. Explore how artists express their understanding of this story, and encourage pupils to do the same. The websites listed below are active at the time of writing.

- www.biblical-art.com > biblical subject > New Testament > gospels > Gospels, Jesus, public ministry: preparations
- www.biblepicturegallery.com
- www.heqigallery.com (browse galleries)

Symbols used in this story

- Footprints: following where someone else leads.
- Nets: the net of God's love. Simon (later known as Peter) was called to become a 'fisher of people'.

Reflective activity

In a quiet area, mark a pair of footprints on the floor, large enough to take the biggest pupil's feet. If they wish, pupils can place their feet inside the footprints and think about what it would mean to follow Jesus. Some teachings of Jesus can be displayed on attractive backgrounds.

Alternatively, pupils can stand on the footprints and think about who they follow. Do these people set an example worth following?

Assessment

Assess the pupils' understanding by observing them replaying the script, or ask them to talk about the display or write about it.

Background information and understanding the story

Jesus was a Jewish teacher who taught by word and example about friendship with God and living by God's values.

The first four disciples were fishermen; they worked on the Sea of Galilee. They had probably already met Jesus when they were called to follow him (John 1:35–42). Other disciples were from very different walks of life: for example, Matthew was a tax collector.

Jesus gathered a band of twelve men. They followed him for three years, witnessing his miracles and teaching and sharing daily life with him. Women also followed Jesus (Luke 8:1–3).

The disciples left their families to follow Jesus. Families lived together in those days, with aunties and uncles, grandparents and cousins. Although it would have been difficult for them, the close families of the disciples would have been looked after by this wider family. We also know that the disciples returned to their homes on occasions.

There are over two billion Christians in the world today.

Useful websites

The websites listed below are active at the time of writing.

- www.textweek.com/art/art.htm > Aaron to Dreams > Disciples
- www.en.wikipedia.org > search 'twelve apostles'

Script 1

Unpacking the bag

My bag is light brown, the colour of sand,
the sand you find on a shore near a lake.
In my bag is water that forms a lake
and fish that swim in the water.
In my bag there are boats
and fishermen that catch fish.
In my bag are nets used to catch fish.
In my bag is a teacher who invites people to follow him.

The story

The story starts on the sand *(place bag and smooth)*. The sand is at the edge of a lake *(place blue cloth)*. In the lake are fish *(place fish)*. On the lake sail two boats *(place boats)*. In the boats are fishermen who work to catch fish *(place two men in each boat)*. The fishermen throw their nets into the water and wait for the fish to swim in *(place nets in men's hands)*.

Beside the lake walks the teacher. He knows these fishermen—he has met them before *(place Jesus on bag)*. He calls to the men in the first boat to leave their nets and follow him *(lower nets)*. The men listen to him and follow *(remove two men from one boat and place them following Jesus)*. The three men walk on, leaving footprints in the sand *(move all three figures)* and soon they come to another boat. Again the teacher calls the fishermen to follow. They listen to him and leave their nets and follow him *(remove two men from the other boat and place them following Jesus)*.

The five men leave the lake; there are things to learn from the teacher *(move all figures off cloth)*. There are other people he needs to invite to follow him.

You will need
❖ A light brown bag
❖ Blue cloth for water
❖ 5 people: 4 fishermen, 1 Jesus
❖ 2 boats (small open cardboard boxes with a card boat shape stuck to the front of each)
❖ 2 pieces of 'net' (fruit packaging)
❖ Paper fish

Questions
(See also page 11.)

❍ Who is the teacher and what did he teach?
❍ Why did people follow him?
❍ Do people still follow this teacher today?

Reproduced with permission from *Bible Storybags®* published by BRF 2011 (978 0 85746 073 8) www.barnabasinschools.org.uk

THE FOOTPRINTS (JESUS CHOOSES HIS FIRST DISCIPLES)

Older pupils

Script 2

Unpacking the bag

My bag is light brown, the colour of sand.
There is water in my bag that forms a lake,
and fish that swim in the water.
There are men in my bag,
and boats in which they sail.
There are nets in my bag that are used to catch fish.
There is a teacher in my bag,
and the footprints of those who follow him.

The story

Our story starts on the shore…	*Place bag*
where the water laps the sand…	*Smooth*
setting it firm.	
Our story takes place by a lake…	*Place blue cloth*
whose waters are full of fish…	*Add fish*
whose surface is full of boats…	*Place two boats on blue cloth*
A lake where men fish for food to eat.	*Place two people in each boat and add nets to their hands*
Along the shores of the lake comes the teacher.	*Walk Jesus along the sand*
His footprints circle its edge.	*Place footprints*
The footprints stop.	*Stop by first boat*
His voice calls across the water, saying, 'Follow me.' The nets fall…	*Lower nets into boat.* *Take men from boat*
the footprints move on and…	*The three move on*
one becomes three.	

Reproduced with permission from *Bible Storybags®* published by BRF 2011 (978 0 85746 073 8) **www.barnabasinschools.org.uk**

THE FOOTPRINTS (JESUS CHOOSES HIS FIRST DISCIPLES)

The footprints continue to circle the lake.	*Walk the three people to the next boat*
Again they stop.	*Place more footprints*
Once more the voice calls across the water, saying, 'Follow me.' The nets fall...	*Lower nets. Take men from the boat*
the footprints move on and...	*The five move on*
three becomes five.	*Place more footprints*
The footprints move on across the sand...	*Move all figures off the cloth*
out into the world...	*Place more footprints*
into tomorrow. The five becomes twelve...	*Place lots of footprints all over the sand*
the twelve becomes a hundred... the hundred becomes a thousand...	*Place lots more footprints*
the thousand becomes a million...	*Place lots more footprints*

the million becomes billions.
Still the voice calls across the world.
Still the voice says, 'Follow me.'

Questions
(See also page 11.)

- Who is the teacher? What did he teach?
- Why did people follow him?
- Who still invites people to follow today?
- How did the one become so many?

Reproduced with permission from *Bible Storybags®* published by BRF 2011 (978 0 85746 073 8) www.barnabasinschools.org.uk

THE FOOTPRINTS (JESUS CHOOSES HIS FIRST DISCIPLES)

The shepherd

The good shepherd and lost sheep

Using the storybag® in Assembly

To introduce the subject, tell pupils that you have lost something and ask them to help you find it. (Hide something beforehand.) Talk about times when people get lost and what it feels like to be found. With older pupils, talk about times when we 'go astray' (refuse to listen, make wrong choices and get ourselves in trouble or danger); this is a way of talking about a different type of being 'lost'. It's about losing your way in life. Use role-play to demonstrate both types of being lost. Discuss how it matters when someone is lost—even if it is only one person. Introduce the Bible story (see Introduction, page 7).

Present the story using the storybag® or the web version (see pages 47–50) and the biblical material (see page 45).

> **Comment**
> Jesus told this story to communicate God's character and how he cares for each person. Jesus said that God is like a shepherd who is prepared to put himself in danger for just one sheep.

Reflection

Ask pupils to hold up ten fingers, then count down to one, folding a finger down each time. Stop when you get to one: just one sheep mattered. Jesus taught that each person matters to God.

 Prayer (optional)

Thank you, Father God, that you care for each person as if there was only one person instead of billions.

44

Introduce the subject using some of the material from the assembly introduction (see page 44).

Select the appropriate script and turn to pages 9 and 10 to find ways of using it.

Biblical material

Luke 15:1–7 (see also John 10:1–16 and Psalm 23)

All sorts of people came to hear Jesus speak. Even the people that no one else liked came. The unimportant people came. The rejected people came. Jesus showed them that they were important to God and welcomed and loved by him. One day, the religious leaders started complaining about the people that Jesus mixed with. 'These are unimportant and bad people,' they said. 'Why is Jesus spending time with them?' Jesus looked at them sadly and told this story.

'If any of you has a hundred sheep, and one of them gets lost, what will you do? Won't you leave the 99 in the field and go look for the lost sheep until you find it? And when you find it, you will be so glad that you will put it on your shoulder and carry it home. Then you will call in your friends and neighbours and say, "Let's celebrate! I've found my lost sheep."'

Jesus said that that is just what it is like for God when one person who has gone wrong says 'sorry' and comes back. There is a party in heaven when that happens.

Jesus also said that he was the good shepherd. He knows his sheep by name and they know him. He leads them to green grass and cares for them. He will not run away when the wolf comes. He will lay down his life for the sheep.

> **Note:** For a comment on this story, see the assembly section (page 44).

Follow-up activities

(See also pages 11 and 12.) Select from these activities according to the age and aptitude of your pupils.

1. Encourage pupils to listen to music as they reflect on the story. They can express their own ideas and understanding through sound and music. Some suggested pieces are as follows.

- Beethoven's 6th Symphony (Movements 1 and 2)
- Tchaikovsky's 6th Symphony (Finale: Movement 4)
- 'Ode to joy' from Beethoven's 9th Symphony

2. Create a display of this script on a green background. Add two-dimensional versions of the items from the bag. Add questions and comments from the pupils. Sections of the script could act as captions.

3. Enact this story in order to communicate its meaning. Photograph the scenes to create a photostory, and add captions using the script or the pupils' own words. Ask pupils to identify the most important picture and say why it is important. How is this parable relevant for today?

4. Explore what thoughts and feelings might have been experienced by the shepherd or the sheep at different moments. Add thought bubbles and hearts to the display to show them. With younger pupils, the teacher can act as the scribe.

5. Using a plain script (see page 12), colour any words that show you the character of the shepherd. Look for actions, thoughts and speech.

6. Explore how artists express their understanding of this story, and encourage pupils to do the same. The websites listed below are active at the time of writing.

- www.biblical-art.com > biblical subject > New Testament > Gospels, Jesus, public ministry: words of Jesus
- www.biblepicturegallery.com
- www.mccrimmons.com > search 'Jesus our hope'
- www.Jesusmafa.com > posters

Symbols used in this story

- The deep pool of water: trouble (Psalm 69:1–4).
- Scars and blood on the shepherd's hands: sacrificial love (love that costs); hints of the crucifixion.
- Shepherd: God's care, protection and sacrificial love (John 10:1–18).

- Sheep: people, some of whom go astray (make wrong choices).
- Sheepfold: a safe place; being in the presence of God.
- Green fields: meeting people's needs (Psalm 23:1–3).
- Thorny bush: danger; hint of the crown of thorns.
- Being lost: wandering away from God (Luke 15).
- Stream: in this context, it means the water we need for life (Psalm 23:2). Water is also a symbol of eternal life (John 4:13–14).
- Tears: the sadness of God.
- Red drops: blood, the sacrifice and danger involved to rescue people.

Reflective activity

Make a reflective area with a green cloth on a small table. Add the bag with its items. Around the area, have pictures of people from all parts of the world and pictures of crowds. While in the area, pupils can think about the billions of people in the world and how Christians believe that God cares for each one and that each one matters. Add the text 'Each person matters' or 'Each person matters to God'.

In a basket have paper sheep 'bracelets' (photocopy the picture below). Pupils can add their own name to the sheep shape, if they wish, and wear the bracelet as a reminder that each person matters.

Assessment

Assess the pupils' understanding by observing them replaying the script, or ask them to talk about the display or write about it.

Background information and understanding the story

This is a story about God's love for each person, even those who have 'gone astray'. In the Bible, God is often likened to a shepherd and Jesus called himself 'the good shepherd'. He hinted at the crucifixion when he said, 'A good shepherd lays down his life for his sheep.'

Biblical shepherds led sheep rather than driving them. They had to find grass and water for them in a dry land. A shepherd built a sheepfold from rocks to keep the sheep safe. He often slept across the entrance to guard the sheep.

Wolves, lions and bears all presented dangers for sheep (and shepherd), as well as rocks, thorns and chasms.

Useful websites

The websites listed below are active at the time of writing.

- www.reonline.org > infants > Bible
- www.request.org.uk (browse teacher's area)
- www.textweek.com/art/art.htm > Jacob to Mustard Seed > Jesus/Christ > Parables

Reproduced with permission from *Bible Storybags®* published by BRF 2011 (978 0 85746 073 8) www.barnabasinschools.org.uk

Script 1

Unpacking the bag

My bag is green, the colour of grass.
There is blue in my bag, the blue of water on a summer's day.
There is a bush in my bag, sharp and prickly.
There is a deep pool that is dark and dangerous.
There is a shepherd in my bag who looks after his sheep.
There are sheep with soft wool.
There is a sheepfold in my bag—a fence to keep the sheep safe.
There is red in my bag. I wonder what it is for?
There is a party in my bag, for this is a story of joy.

The story

Our story takes place on a green cloth, for this story starts in a field *(place bag and smooth)*. Through the field runs a gentle stream of water *(place ribbon)*. In the field is a shepherd *(place shepherd)* and his sheep *(place sheep)*. To keep the sheep safe, the shepherd builds a sheepfold *(move shepherd, place fold)*. The sheepfold is a fenced place to keep the sheep from harm.

The shepherd leads the sheep to the water *(move shepherd and sheep near water)* and checks for dangers. He finds a deep, dark pool *(place pool, move shepherd)*. The sheep must not go there! He finds a prickly bush *(place bush, move shepherd)*. The sheep must not go there!

At night the shepherd places the sheep in the sheepfold to keep them safe *(place shepherd by fold and place all but one of the sheep in the sheepfold)*. One night he notices one of his sheep is missing *(place one sheep behind the bush)*. One sheep has not come in when called.

The shepherd goes in search of his sheep. He looks in the field *(move shepherd around field)*. The sheep is not there! He looks by the stream *(go to the stream)*. The sheep is not there! He looks in the deep, dark pool *(go to the pool)*. The sheep is not there! Finally, he looks by the prickly bush and finds the sheep caught by its wool *(go to the bush)*. Carefully he lifts out the sheep, and his hands are scratched by the thorns *(add scratches with face paint)*. He carries the sheep home *(place the sheep in the sheepfold)* and throws a party with his friends, for he is glad to have found his sheep that was lost *(throw streamers; give safe party items to children to join in)*.

You will need
- A green bag
- 1 shepherd
- A few toy sheep
- A sheepfold from a play farm (or cut from a small cardboard box)
- A prickly bush (screwed-up green tissue, with some twisted points)
- Shiny blue ribbon for the stream
- A small irregular circle of dark cloth for a deep pool
- Children's red face-paint crayon
- Safe party items (e.g. streamers)

Questions
(See also page 11.)

- Who is the shepherd?
- Who are the sheep?
- Why did the sheep wander off?
- Why did the shepherd look for just one sheep?

Reproduced with permission from *Bible Storybags®* published by BRF 2011 (978 0 85746 073 8) www.barnabasinschools.org.uk

THE SHEPHERD (THE GOOD SHEPHERD AND LOST SHEEP)

Script 2

Unpacking the bag

My bag is green, the colour of grass.
There is blue in my bag, the blue of water on a summer's day.
There is a bush in my bag, sharp and thorny.
There is a pool in my bag, dark and deep and dangerous.
There is a shepherd in my bag who looks after his sheep.
There are sheep in my bag, with soft wool.
There is a sheepfold in my bag—a fence to keep the sheep safe.
There are tears in the bag that glitter like diamonds.
There is blood in my bag, as red as rubies.
There is red in my bag. I wonder what it is for?

The story

This story happens in a field…	*Place bag*
a green place, a beautiful place…	*Smooth*
a place where you can stop and think.	
A stream runs through the field…	*Place ribbon*
making shallow pools of water…	*Run finger down it*
where you can splash and play and drink.	
There is another pool in the field.	*Place pool*
It is deep and dark and dangerous.	
There are bushes on the other side of the stream…	*Place bush on other side of stream*
thorny bushes, spiky bushes, prickly bushes; bushes that scratch and scar and tangle.	*Touch and withdraw quickly*

Reproduced with permission from *Bible Storybags*® published by BRF 2011 (978 0 85746 073 8) www.barnabasinschools.org.uk

THE SHEPHERD (THE GOOD SHEPHERD AND LOST SHEEP)

You will need

✤ A green bag
✤ 1 shepherd
✤ A few toy sheep
✤ A sheepfold from a play farm (or cut down a small cardboard box to make a shallow sheep pen)
✤ A prickly bush (screwed-up green tissue, with some tissue twisted into points)
✤ Shiny blue ribbon for the stream
✤ A small irregular circle of dark cloth for a deep pool
✤ Children's red face-paint crayon
✤ Silver paper tear shapes
✤ Shiny red paper droplets

Note: A version of this script originally appeared in *Firm Foundations Book 2: Exploring Christianity at Foundation Level*, available from www.rmep.co.uk.

A shepherd is in this field.	*Place shepherd*
He knows every part of it: he knows the soft green grass…	*Indicate grass*
he knows the gentle stream…	*Indicate stream*
he knows the deep, dark pool…	*Circle pool*
he knows the thorny bush.	*Touch and withdraw*

He knows them all, for he has been here many times.

He carefully builds a sheepfold…	*Place sheepfold*
a place where the sheep are safe: safe from the deep, dark pool…	*Circle pool*
safe from the thorny bush…	*Touch and withdraw*

safe from anything that might want to hurt them.

The sheep eat the grass in the soft, green field…	*Place sheep near stream*
they drink the water from the gentle stream. They do not go near the deep, dark pool…	*Indicate pool and shake head*
they do not go near the thorny bush…	*Indicate bush and shake head*

for those places are dangerous.

At night the shepherd gathers his sheep…	*Place most sheep in fold*
into the fold to keep them safe. But one of them is missing!	*Place one sheep behind bush*
The shepherd's tears fall like diamonds…	*Drop 'tears'*

for he loves his sheep that is lost.

Reproduced with permission from *Bible Storybags*® published by BRF 2011 (978 0 85746 073 8) www.barnabasinschools.org.uk

THE SHEPHERD (THE GOOD SHEPHERD AND LOST SHEEP)

He looks in the soft, green field for his missing sheep…	*Move shepherd around*
he searches the gentle stream…	*Go to stream*
he goes to the deep, dark pool…	*Go to pool*
but there is no sign of his sheep. He crosses the gentle stream…	*Cross stream*

calling his sheep by name in the night.
But all is silent.

At last he reaches the thorny bush…	*Reach bush*

and out of the bush comes a tired cry,
for the sheep is trapped on the thorns.

The shepherd reaches deep into the bush…	*Push hands into bush*
but the bush bites back with its thorns.	*Withdraw hands quickly*
Blood red as rubies stains the ground.	*Scatter red drops*
Deeper and deeper go his searching hands, until he touches the woolly coat…	*Lift out sheep*

and tenderly lifts his sheep out.

Carrying the sheep in his strong, safe arms, he wades the gentle stream…	*Cross stream*
he crosses the soft, green grass…	*Cross grass*
and places the sheep in the fold.	*Put sheep in fold*
The shepherd smiles at his blood-stained hands…	*Make red marks on inside palms*

and looks at his sheep, safe in the fold,
and inside his heart is a quiet joy
for he has found his sheep that was lost.

Questions
(See also page 11.)

- Who is the shepherd?
- Who are the sheep?
- Why did the sheep wander off?
- What does it cost the shepherd to rescue the sheep?

Reproduced with permission from *Bible Storybags®* published by BRF 2011 (978 0 85746 073 8) www.barnabasinschools.org.uk

THE SHEPHERD (THE GOOD SHEPHERD AND LOST SHEEP)

The road of choices

The good Samaritan

⌣ ⌣

Using the storybag® in Assembly

To introduce the subject, give children a variety of choices to make—for example, choosing between a red or blue pencil, or two types of sticker. (Use cheap but safe items that the children can keep.)

When we make a choice, we say 'yes' to one thing and 'no' to another. We often find out things about a person by the choices they make. What applies to ordinary choices also applies to the big choices in life. Sometimes we have to choose how to behave. When we say 'yes' to caring and 'no' to bullying, it tells other people what we are like as a person.

Ask four pupils to hold cards, each with a positive behaviour and a YES on one side and the opposite behaviour and a NO on the other. The rest of the school only sees the positive side and has to guess what is on the other side.

YES	NO
Telling the truth	Telling lies

Introduce the Bible story (see Introduction, page 7).

Present the story using the storybag® or the web version (see pages 54–57) and the biblical material (see page 52).

Comment

This is a story of radical kindness that ignores all barriers of race or religion. It is not just about being 'nice', for the man who helps puts himself in danger for an enemy. Jesus often told stories that challenged the ideas of his day.

Reflection

Show a series of images of different 'roads' (available online). Follow this with different scenarios, such as a playground, shopping, and watching TV. Anywhere can be a 'road of choices': it does not have to be an actual road. The road of choices is simply the place where we make a decision about how we will behave.

Prayer *(optional)*

Dear God, as we face difficult choices in life, help us to learn from wrong choices and give us a sense of your presence through all the rights and wrongs, the ups and the downs.

Using the storybag® in RE

Introduce the subject using some of the material from the assembly introduction (see page 51).

Select the appropriate script and turn to pages 9 and 10 to find ways of using it.

Biblical material

Luke 10:25–37

One day, a man came to Jesus with an important question. 'Who is my neighbour?' he asked. Jesus did not give him an answer; instead he told this story.

A man was walking from the city of Jerusalem, where the temple was, to the town of Jericho. On the way, he was attacked and beaten by robbers who left him lying in the road. Shortly after this, a priest came by, a religious leader. He saw the injured man but did not help. Instead he passed by on the other side. A little while later, another man walked down the road. He, too, was a religious leader (a Levite, someone who helped at the temple) but he also passed by on the other side. Later that day, an enemy, called a Samaritan, walked along the road. He saw the injured man and stopped to help. He bandaged the man's wounds, put him on his donkey and took him to the town. When they arrived, the Samaritan paid for the man's care and offered to pay more.

'Which one acted as neighbour?' asked Jesus.

'The Samaritan,' replied the man.

'Go and behave in the same way,' said Jesus.

> **Note:** For a comment on this story, see the assembly section (page 51).

Follow-up activities

(See also pages 11 and 12.) Select from these activities according to the age and aptitude of your pupils.

1. Create a display using a brown background and adding two-dimensional versions of the items from the bag. Add questions and comments from the pupils. Sections of the script could act as captions.

The coins symbolize care. Write examples on the back of paper 'coins' of how people can care today.

Staple them to the display by one edge only, so that they can be lifted up. Create a parallel road to represent the journey through life. The choices people face today can be written on the road.

2. Write a poem or a piece of prose called 'The song of the rocks' or 'The song of the road'. What did the rocks and road see? What would they comment on?

3. Imagine one of the men who passed by looking back and seeing the enemy helping the injured man. How would he have felt? How might this experience have changed him?

4. Discuss what the characters would have been thinking at various points in the story. Draw outlines of heads for the various characters. Inside the outlines, write and draw a collage of thoughts and images that might have been going through the characters' heads in the course of this journey. When do thoughts like these go through people's heads today?

5. Explore how artists express their understanding of this story, and encourage pupils to do the same. The websites listed below are active at the time of writing.

- www.nationalgallery.org.uk > search 'good Samaritan'
- www.heqigallery.com (browse galleries)
- www.biblical-art.com > biblical subject > New Testament > Gospels, Jesus, public ministry: words of Jesus > parables
- www.biblepicturegallery.com
- www.Jesusmafa.com > mini posters

6. Divide a page into two columns headed 'Characters' and 'Feelings'. Write a list of characters from the story on one side. On the opposite side, write the emotions (in any order) that may have been experienced by those characters. Underline each character in a different colour.

Select one character and link them to the emotions you think they experienced in the story by drawing lines between the character and the emotions, in the correct colour for that person. Repeat for the other characters. (See diagram below for examples.)

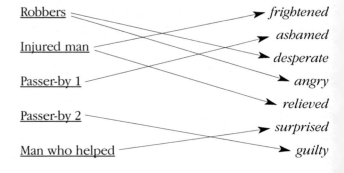

Symbols used in this story

- The road: life's journey. In this case, the events along the road force people to make choices.
- The rocks: danger (because evil people hid in the shadows).
- Coins: a practical expression of care.

Reflective activity

Cover a small table with an attractive cloth, and add the bag. In a basket, place some safe scissors and some small pieces of paper that you would normally throw away because they are damaged. Give pupils a few moments to turn a piece of paper into something beautiful by folding and cutting, and display their work around the reflective area. For younger pupils, replace scissors with crayons to make patterns.

Making a wrong choice is not the end of the matter. People can learn from their mistakes. A rip can become part of a beautiful pattern. Wrong choices, combined with forgiveness, can change people for the better: they may decide never to make that wrong choice again.

Assessment

Assess the pupils' understanding by observing them replaying the script, or ask them to talk about the display or write about it.

Background information and understanding the story

The road between Jerusalem and Jericho is very steep and was infested with bandits.

The priest and the Levite (a helper from the temple) may have been worried about being attacked themselves, or concerned about touching a dead body, which would have made them ritually impure and unable to do their duties at the temple. However, the Old Testament makes it clear that compassion outweighs other concerns and God is more concerned with love than sacrifice.

There had been a feud between the Samaritan and Jewish people for over 400 years. The Samaritans were seen as impure owing to their intermarriage with other nations and because they did not worship at the Jerusalem temple.

Useful websites

The websites listed below are active at the time of writing.

- www.reonline.org > infants > Bible
- www.request.org.uk (browse teacher's area)
- www.textweek.com/art/art.htm > Jacob to Mustard Seed > Jesus/Christ > Parables

Younger pupils

Questions
(See also page 11.)

* Who are the people in this story?
* Why did some people ignore the injured man?
* Why do you think the road is called the road of choices?

Script 1

Unpacking the bag

My bag is brown, the colour of earth.
There are rocks in my bag, hard and rough.
There is a road in my bag: it is the road of choices.
There are robbers in my bag, who hide among the rocks.
There are four travellers in my bag; each travels alone.
There are coins in my bag, coins for caring.

The story

Our story takes place on a brown cloth, the colour of earth *(place bag and smooth)*. Across our cloth runs a road *(place road)*. This is the road of choices. Everyone who walks along this road makes a choice *(run your finger down road)*. There are rocks on the road *(place rocks near road)* and there are robbers who hide behind the rocks *(place robbers)*. They are waiting to attack!

The first traveller walks down the road, and when he reaches the rocks the robbers attack and leave him injured on the road *(robbers attack the traveller and then move off the cloth)*.

A second traveller walks down the road *(walk man two down the road)*. He sees the injured man and makes a choice: he crosses over and walks on *(cross over and walk off cloth)*. He does not help.

A third traveller walks down the road *(walk man three down the road)*. He sees the injured man and makes a choice: he, too, crosses over and walks on *(cross over and walk off cloth)*. He does not help.

Finally, a fourth man walks along the road. He is an enemy *(walk man four down the road)*. He sees the injured man and makes a choice: he stops to help. He carries the injured man to the town and pays for his care *(walk man four and injured man down road together; drop coins on cloth)*.

Each person made a choice. Their choices show us what sort of people they are. We, too, make choices as we walk through life. Our choices show what sort of people we are.

Reproduced with permission from *Bible Storybags*® published by BRF 2011 (978 0 85746 073 8) www.barnabasinschools.org.uk

THE ROAD OF CHOICES (THE GOOD SAMARITAN)

Script 2

Unpacking the bag

My bag is brown, the colour of earth.
There are rocks in my bag, hard and rough.
There is a road in my bag, the road of choices.
There are robbers in my bag, who hide among the rocks.
There are four travellers in my bag; each travels alone.
There are coins in my bag, coins for caring.

The story

Our story takes place on a rough brown cloth…	*Place bag and smooth*
the colour of earth, hard-packed from the feet of many travellers.	
A road slices through the land…	*Place road*
cutting its way across the hills, all the way from the temple to the town.	*Point to two ends of road*
It is the road of choices.	
There are rocks along the road…	*Place rocks near road*
hard and jagged, rocks where people can hide. The rocks cast their shadow over the road, the shadow of fear.	
There are robbers on the road.	*Place robbers behind rocks*
They hide behind the rocks, waiting for a victim.	
There are four travellers. Each travels alone.	*Hold up four travellers*

You will need
* A brown bag
* A brown ribbon for the road
* Screwed-up brown paper for rocks
* 6 people: 4 travellers, 2 robbers
* A few coins

Note: A version of this script originally appeared in *REthinking Book 9: God, Faith and the Classroom*, available from www.stapleford-centre.org.

Reproduced with permission from *Bible Storybags*® published by BRF 2011 (978 0 85746 073 8) www.barnabasinschools.org.uk

THE ROAD OF CHOICES (THE GOOD SAMARITAN)

Older pupils

The first traveller walks along
the hard-packed road...

Place traveller on the road

the road of choices.
He is travelling from
the temple to the town.
He reaches the rocks...

*Robbers jump on man when he
is halfway along*

and the robbers attack.
They beat his body,
they steal his clothes,
they leave him dying on the road.

Lay man down on the road

The robbers have made their choice.

Place robbers off cloth

A second man walks along
the hard-packed road...

Move second man along road

the road of choices.
He too is travelling from the temple
to the town.
He sees the dying man and does not help...

Pause by injured man

instead he crosses over and hurries on.

Walk on and place off the cloth

He has made his choice.

A third man walks along
the hard-packed road...

Move third man along road

the road of choices.
He is travelling from the temple to the town.
He sees the injured man and does not help...
instead he crosses over and hurries on.
He has made his choice.

Finally, an enemy walks along
the hard-packed road...

Place fourth man on road

the road of choices.
He is travelling to the same town.

Indicate end of road

He sees the man and stops to help.

Pause man

Reproduced with permission from *Bible Storybags*® published by BRF 2011 (978 0 85746 073 8) www.barnabasinschools.org.uk

THE ROAD OF CHOICES (THE GOOD SAMARITAN)

He bandages his wounds
and carries him.

*The two men travel down
the road and off the cloth*

He, too, has made his choice.

When he reaches the town he pays
for the man's care...

Drop coins

and offers more.

The road of choices has done its work.

Lift road

The robbers chose violence...

Lift robbers

two chose to cross over...

Lift travellers

the enemy chose to help.

Lift traveller

The choices show us what sort of
people they were.

We all travel through life,
walking a hard road of choices.

Lift road

There may not be robbers...

Lift robbers

there may not be rocks...

Lift rocks

but there will be choices,
choices that show what sort of person we are.

Point to self

Questions
(See also page 11.)

- Why do you think the road is called the road of choices?
- What choices do people make?
- How do their choices show us what they are like?
- How do you think these people felt about their choices?

Reproduced with permission from *Bible Storybags®* published by BRF 2011 (978 0 85746 073 8) www.barnabasinschools.org.uk

The seed

The mustard seed

Using the storybag® in Assembly

To introduce the subject, talk about things that start small and grow big. If possible, ask a parent to visit with a young baby. Talk about the potential in the baby. Place the baby alongside children and an adult and compare their sizes. Talk about what the baby can do now and might be able to do when an adult.

Explain that today's story is about something that started small and grew big. Introduce the Bible story (see Introduction, page 7).

Present the story using the storybag® or the web version (see pages 61–64) and the biblical material (see page 59).

> **Comment**
> Christians believe that the kingdom of God is not a place, but is made up of all the people who accept God as their king. It started small (with just twelve men), then grew and grew. Christians believe that people who accept God as king should live in the way that God wants, showing love and care for others, bringing peace and justice.

Reflection

Show pictures of the staff or yourself as babies (with permission) or use a series of baby pictures. Ask pupils to look at baby pictures and think about how small a baby is. That tiny baby could become anything! Lots of things start small but have huge potential.

Prayer *(optional)*

Dear Lord, thank you for those first followers who had the courage to follow Jesus even when others dismissed him as just the son of a carpenter. Help us to live by the kingdom values of love, justice and peace.

Using the storybag® in RE

Introduce the subject using some of the material from the assembly introduction (see page 58).

Select the appropriate script and turn to pages 9 and 10 to find ways of using it.

Biblical material

Matthew 13:31–32

The kingdom of God is like a mustard seed that a person takes and plants in his or her garden. The seed is tiny—the smallest seed—but it grows into a large garden plant in which birds can nest.

> **Note:** For a comment on this story, see the assembly section (page 58).

Follow-up activities

(See also pages 11 and 12.) Select from these activities according to the age and aptitude of your pupils.

1. Create a three-dimensional display of this story on a table, using the items from the bag. Add labels and the script in a folder and a children's Bible opened at the appropriate page. Encourage the pupils to ask questions and add comments, which can be displayed in a toast rack.

2. Encourage pupils to explore this story in dance and movement, expressing their own ideas and understanding. For example, use uncurling, growing movements for the seed. Add the other characters from the script and their movements: walking, dancing and so on. Perform the dance while the script is read.

3. Make an autocue for this story, using key words in the correct order. What are the key words? Why are they important? Retell the story using an autocue.

4. Create a modern parable that will communicate the same message. What other object could stand for the kingdom increasing in size slowly?

5. Create a haiku poem about the seed growing to a plant. A haiku is a three-lined poem with counted syllables:
- Line 1: five syllables
- Line 2: seven syllables
- Line 3: five syllables

Sum up the essential message of the parable in the poem.

6. Explore some other parables about the kingdom. Create a diagram showing how they link. For example:

- The yeast: Matthew 13:33
- The hidden treasure: Matthew 13:44
- The seed growing secretly: Mark 4:26–29

Symbols used in this story

- The seed: growth and the power of God. The seed grows quietly and unnoticed.
- The plant: growth and the size of the kingdom. Growth is quiet but steady owing to the power in the seed (its potential).

Reflective activity

Cover a table in a green cloth and add the bag for pupils to replay. Display pictures of seeds and the plants they grow into, and magazine pictures of children and adults. Use the pictures to help children reflect on their own potential. Have paper and pencils available in a basket for pupils to write or draw small things that grow into something big—for example, acorns to oak trees.

Assessment

Assess the pupils' understanding by observing them replaying the script, or ask them to talk about the display or write about it.

Background information and understanding the story

The kingdom of God is also known as the kingdom of heaven. Christians believe that it is an invisible kingdom where God's values, such as love, justice and peace, prevail. It's made up of all the people who accept God as their king and try to live by the values of the kingdom. As more people do this, the kingdom grows, but it grows quietly—like a seed turning into a plant. It started with just a few people and there are now over two billion Christians.

Christians believe that the kingdom is something that is already here (people who already accept God as king and try to live by his values) and it is also still to come. That is why, in the Lord's Prayer, they pray, 'your kingdom come'. It is a prayer that kingdom values will one day become universal, and evil will disappear.

Mustard has a small seed but grows into a large plant.

Useful websites

The websites listed below are active at the time of writing.

- ✿ www.textweek.com/art/art.htm > Jacob to Mustard Seed > Mustard Seed
- ✿ www.en.wikipedia.org > search 'mustard seed'

Script 1

Unpacking the bag

My bag is brown, the colour of earth.
There is a sun in my bag that warms the earth, and rain that waters it.
There is a bird in my bag, looking for somewhere to nest.
There are children in my bag who like to play and dance.
There are men and women who are busy working.
There is a seed in my bag, so small you can hardly see it.
There are plants in my bag of different sizes.

The story

Our story takes place on a deep brown cloth, the colour of earth freshly dug *(place bag)*. A seed falls on the earth, but it is so small that no one sees it *(place seed and bunch cloth around it)*. The rain falls and the sun shines *(use rain stick, drop raindrops, hold up sun)* and the seed grows into a small plant *(add a small plant on top of seed)*. But it is still so small that people do not notice it *(place people near plant)*. The children play *(move children in play)* and the men and women work *(move adults)*, not realizing that the plant is there.

The rain falls and the sun shines *(use rain stick, drop raindrops, hold up sun)* and the plant grows *(replace small plant with a medium one)*. Now the children notice the plant. They dance around it *(dance children)*, and the men and women walk round it as they work *(move adults around it)*.

The rain falls and the sun shines *(use rain stick, drop raindrops, hold up sun)* and the plant continues to grow *(replace plant with large one)*. Now *everyone* notices the plant. It is so big, they cannot ignore it! The children play games around it *(move children as if playing)*, and the men and women rest in its shade *(stand adults by plant)*. The birds of the air make their nests in it *(place bird in plant)*.

You will need
- A brown bag
- Yellow paper sun
- Rain stick or shaker
- Silver paper raindrops
- 4 people: 1 man, 1 woman, 2 children
- Rolled black tissue paper for the seed
- 3 'plants' of different sizes (crumpled green tissue paper)
- Paper bird

Questions
(See also page 11.)

- Why did no one notice the seed at first?
- Do we often ignore small things?
- Why did they all notice it in the end?

Script 2

You will need

You will need
- A brown bag
- Yellow paper sun
- Rain stick or shaker
- Silver paper raindrops
- 4 people: 1 man, 1 woman, 2 children
- Rolled black tissue paper for the seed
- 3 'plants' of different sizes (crumpled green tissue paper)
- Paper bird

Unpacking the bag

My bag is brown, the colour of earth.
There is a sun in my bag that warms the earth.
There is rain in my bag that waters the earth.
There is a bird in my bag, looking for somewhere to nest.
There are children in my bag who like to play and dance.
There are men in my bag who work in the fields.
There are women in my bag, busy all day.
There is a seed in my bag, so small you can hardly see it.
There are plants in my bag, one too small to notice, one too big to ignore and one in between.

The story

Our story takes place on a deep brown cloth…	*Place cloth and smooth*
the colour of wet earth, freshly dug.	
Our story starts with a seed…	*Put seed between finger and thumb and then put it down outside the cloth*
that everyone ignored: a small seed…	*Use finger and thumb to indicate size, getting smaller and smaller*
a tiny seed, the smallest seed of all.	
Our story ends with a plant…	*Pick up large plant and put it down again outside the cloth*
that could not be ignored: a great plant…	*Use hands and arms to indicate size*
a tall plant, the largest plant of all.	

Reproduced with permission from *Bible Storybags*® published by BRF 2011 (978 0 85746 073 8) www.barnabasinschools.org.uk

THE SEED (THE MUSTARD SEED)

The tiny seed falls on the dark, wet earth.	*Pick up seed and 'plant' it on the cloth*
Everyone ignores it: it is too small to notice.	*Use finger and thumb to indicate size*
Only the earth welcomes it…	*Bunch up the fabric around it*
with its soil. The men tread on it on the way to the fields…	*Walk man by it*
children dance on it as they play…	*Dance children over it*
women walk on it in the busy day.	*Walk woman by it*
Day after day the sun warms the seed.	*Hold up sun*
Day after day the rain waters it.	*Use rain stick, drop raindrops*
The seed grows into a small plant…	*Place a small plant on top of the seed*
but no one notices: it is too small.	*Use finger and thumb to indicate size*
The men nearly crush it as they walk to the fields…	*Walk man by it*
the children almost break it as they dance and play…	*Dance children round it*
the women brush past it in the busy day.	*Walk woman by it*
No one sees it.	
Day after day the sun warms the plant.	*Hold up sun*
Day after day the rain waters it.	*Use rain stick, drop raindrops*
The plant grows.	*Replace small plant with medium plant*
The men pass it on the way to the fields…	*Walk man round it*

Reproduced with permission from *Bible Storybags®* published by BRF 2011 (978 0 85746 073 8) www.barnabasinschools.org.uk

THE SEED (THE MUSTARD SEED)

children dance near it as they play…	*Dance children round it*
women walk round it in the busy day.	*Move woman round it*
They notice the plant.	
Day after day the sun warms the plant.	*Hold up sun*
Day after day the rain waters it.	*Use rain stick, drop raindrops*
The plant grows and grows until it becomes a great plant…	*Replace medium plant with large plant*
a tall plant…	*Use hands to indicate size*
the largest plant of all.	
The men and women rest in its shade…	*Rest man and woman by it*
children dance around it as they play…	*Children play*
the birds of the air come and make their nest in it.	*Place bird in plant*
No one ignores it: it is too big.	*Indicate size*
Such is the kingdom.	

Questions
(See also page 11.)

- What is the seed?
- Why did no one notice it at first?
- What is the kingdom?

Reproduced with permission from *Bible Storybags®* published by BRF 2011 (978 0 85746 073 8) www.barnabasinschools.org.uk

THE SEED (THE MUSTARD SEED)

The box

The treasure in the field

Using the storybag® in Assembly

To introduce the subject, create a treasure hunt around the hall with clues and treasure at the end. You could have a treasure map on a flipchart. A few pupils could take part with others, reading the map and clues. Talk about different types of treasure. Include the idea that people can be a 'treasure'. Ask teachers to nominate pupils who have been a real 'treasure'. Select pupils to be diamonds, rubies, emeralds and so on (present them with suitable shiny foil badges).

Explain that today's story is all about treasure—a very unusual treasure. Introduce the Bible story (see biblical material and note for teachers on page 66).

Present the story using the storybag® or the web version (see pages 68–71) and the biblical material (see page 66).

> **Comment**
> This is a story about a treasure found in a field. It is a story about worth and value. For Christians, the greatest treasure is a friendship with God and things such as love, hope, peace and justice. That friendship and those invisible treasures are at the heart of the idea of the kingdom of God (see background information for more details). This story can help pupils to reflect on the intangibles of life that give it value—the things that are truly worth everything.

Reflection

Use the jewels from the bag as a focus for this reflection. Pupils can speak each line, holding up a 'jewel'.

Diamonds sparkle, but hope is worth more.
Rubies glow, but peace is precious.
Emeralds shine, but friendship is more important.
Silver glistens, but justice is more valuable.
Gold shimmers, but love outshines them all.

 ### Prayer *(optional)*

Lord God, as we change and grow, help us to remember what is really important in life and not to trade the real treasures for lesser ones.

Introduce the subject using some of the material from the assembly introduction (see page 65).

Select the appropriate script and turn to pages 9 and 10 to find ways of using it.

Biblical material

Matthew 13:44

Jesus said, 'The kingdom of heaven is like what happens when someone finds treasure hidden in a field and buries it again. A person like that is happy and goes and sells everything in order to buy that field.'

Note for teachers

Explore relationships and values such as love, justice and peace as 'treasures'. You may wish also to explore the idea of 'treasures in heaven' (Matthew 6:19–21). Talk with children about what 'treasures in heaven' might mean. (The rest of the Sermon on the Mount, Matthew 5—7, gives some clues. For example, it is about giving to those in need, love, faithfulness and so on.) Make some 'jewels', label them appropriately and put them in a treasure box.

> **Note:** For a comment on this story, see the assembly section (page 65).

Follow-up activities

(See also pages 11 and 12.) Select from these activities according to the age and aptitude of your pupils.

1. Present the story as a puppet drama. Write a script and assess afterwards how well the drama communicated the meaning of the story. You could use paper bags or paper plates as puppets.

2. Create a display using a brown background with brightly coloured jewel shapes and coins as a border. Add two-dimensional versions of items from the bag, plus questions and pupil comments. Add a three-dimensional treasure box with a lift-up lid. Inside, pupils can write their own suggestions for what the treasure might be.

3. Concentrate on the sounds in the story and use them to create a poem with rhythm and pattern. Find lots of different sound words to describe what happens, then put them together to form a poem. Make sure your poem communicates the message of the story. Sounds might include footsteps, an echoing ring and so on.

4. Imagine that the main character in the story has been invited on to a chat show. What would you want to ask him? Create the questions for the show, then enact the chat show. What does this parable have to say to people today? Discuss different types of riches and treasure.

5. Look up the parable of the valuable pearl (Matthew 13:45–46). How does this parable relate to the parable of the hidden treasure? Create an illustrated book of the parable of the valuable pearl that will communicate its message to younger children.

6. Role-play the man phoning his best friend and telling him what he is about to do. How would the friend react? What arguments might the friend use to dissuade him? The dialogue can be written by older pupils.

Symbols used in this story

☺ Field: the world.
☺ Treasure: the kingdom of God/values of the kingdom.
☺ Money or jewels: material wealth.

Reflective activity

Place a treasure box in the middle of a circle of children. Give each child a 'jewel' and ask them to think of things that are 'treasures' for them—not toys or jewels or money, but relationships (including the relationship with God for some), special times, love, joy, peace and so on. When they have thought of something that is worth a lot but is not valuable in monetary terms, they can add their 'jewel' to the box. They do not have to say anything.

Assessment

Assess the pupils' understanding by observing them replaying the script, or ask them to talk about the display or write about it.

Background information and understanding the story

This is a story about finding something so valuable that it is worth everything. That something is described as the 'kingdom of God', which is essentially a relationship with God built around a set of values (such as love, peace and justice). These values and this relationship make up an invisible treasure that is worth everything to possess. For more background information on the kingdom of God, see pages 59–60.

The early Christians often did have to give up everything for their faith. Persecution often meant fleeing an area, leaving behind businesses and homes. This is still true today for Christians in some parts of the world.

Burying treasure was a normal way of keeping it safe in the days before banks and when houses had little security.

Useful websites

The websites listed below are active at the time of writing.

- www.textweek.com/art/art.htm > Jacob to Mustard Seed > Jesus/Christ > Parables
- www.biblical-art.com > biblical subject > New Testament > Gospels, Jesus, public ministry: words of Jesus
- www.biblepicturegallery.com
- www.sermons4kids.com > art by Henry Martin, scroll to PowerPoint slides

Younger pupils

You will need

❖ A brown bag
❖ Jewels (shiny foil paper over plastic shapes)
❖ Small treasure box
❖ 3 people
❖ Some coins

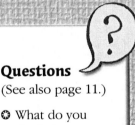

Questions
(See also page 11.)

✪ What do you think the treasure was?
✪ I wonder why the man sells everything he has?

Script 1

Unpacking the bag

My bag is brown, the colour of earth.
There are people in my bag who dig the ground.
There is a person in my bag who finds a treasure.
There are jewels in my bag, but they are not the treasure.
There is money is my bag, but it is not the treasure.
There is treasure in my bag that is worth everything.

The story

Our story starts in a field *(place bag and smooth)*. In the field, people dig the earth *(place men)*. Suddenly, one man's spade hits something hard *(single knock)*. He kneels down to see what it is. He brushes the earth away *(make brushing gesture)* and sees a treasure box *(place box on bag near man)*. The man opens the lid and looks inside *(open and close the lid and gasp, but do not let the children see inside)*. Inside is the greatest treasure in the world.

What is inside? Is it jewels? *(show 'jewels' and drop them on one corner of the bag)*. Is it money? *(show coins and drop them)*. The man hides the box *(place under bag)* and goes away and sells everything he has to get some money to buy the field. Now he has no house *(shake head)*, no chairs *(shake head)* and no bed to sleep on *(shake head)*. He buys the field with the money he got by selling his house and bed and chairs *(drop money)*.

When the field is his, he digs up the box *(bring out the box and place it on the bag)* and looks at the treasure inside *(open the box, gasp, but do not let the children see inside)*. He has sold everything he has to buy it. He has no house *(shake head)*, he has no chairs or bed *(shake head)*, he has nothing *(shake head)*, but when he looks at the treasure *(open and close box)* he knows it was worth it. It is worth everything.

Reproduced with permission from *Bible Storybags®* published by BRF 2011 (978 0 85746 073 8) **www.barnabasinschools.org.uk**

THE BOX (THE TREASURE IN THE FIELD)

Script 2

Unpacking the bag

My bag is brown, the colour of earth.
There are people in my bag who dig the ground.
There is a person in my bag who finds a treasure.
There are jewels in my bag, that some call treasure.
There is money is my bag, that some call treasure.
There is real treasure in my bag that is worth everything.

The story

Our story takes place on a brown cloth, for our story starts in a field.	*Place and smooth cloth*
Our story ends with a box, a treasure box.	*Place treasure box on cloth*
It contains the greatest treasure in the world.	
Did the treasure box contain… red rubies…	*Drop jewels on one side of cloth*
green emeralds… sparkling diamonds… glittering gold… shining silver? Did it contain money?	*Drop coins*
We do not know.	
The box sleeps in the field beneath the soil.	*Place box under the corner of the cloth*
The people who work above it do not know it is there.	*Place people on the cloth*
The box sleeps beneath the soil…	*Touch the box*
silently guarding its treasure.	*Touch lips*

You will need
- A brown bag
- Jewels (shiny foil paper over plastic shapes)
- Small treasure box
- 3 people
- Some coins
- A baking tray for a sound effect

Reproduced with permission from *Bible Storybags*® published by BRF 2011 (978 0 85746 073 8) www.barnabasinschools.org.uk

THE BOX (THE TREASURE IN THE FIELD)

The treasure box sleeps on…	*Place one person near box*
until one day a man digs nearby. His spade rings on its lid…	*Single knock on the baking tray*
and the sound echoes round the field. The man with the spade kneels and brushes the soil from the lid.	*Bring out the box*
He opens the box and sees the treasure within…	*Open lid, gasp, do not show pupils*

the greatest treasure in the world.

Did the treasure box contain… red rubies…	*Drop jewels on one side of cloth*
green emeralds… sparkling diamonds… glittering gold… shining silver? Did it contain money?	*Drop coins*

We do not know.

Quietly he closes the lid…	*Close lid gently*
quickly he buries the box.	*Cover box again*
He returns home to sell everything he has…	*Remove man*

to buy the field where the box
lies buried.

Meanwhile, the people still work in the field…	*Walk people around field*

unaware that beneath their feet lies
the greatest treasure in the world.

Reproduced with permission from *Bible Storybags*® published by BRF 2011 (978 0 85746 073 8) www.barnabasinschools.org.uk

THE BOX (THE TREASURE IN THE FIELD)

The man with the spade…	*Bring back first man*
has no home.	*Shake head*
He has no goods…	*Shake head*
He has nothing!	*Shake head, open hands*
He has sold everything he has to get the money to buy the field…	*Add another coin to the cloth*
and now it is his.	

Carefully he digs beneath the soil…	*Flip back cloth to reveal box*
until his spade rings on the box once more.	*Knock on the baking tray*
He opens the lid and sees the treasure within…	*Open, gasp, but do not show*
and knows that he was right to sell his home…	*Nod head*
to sell his goods…	*Nod head*
to sell everything he had to possess it.	*Nod head*

No more will the box sleep in the field.	*Lift box*
No more will people walk over it.	*Lift people*

The box is awake…
it has shown its worth.
It is worth everything.

Questions
(See also page 11.)

- What would be the greatest treasure in the world?
- Why does the man sell everything he has?
- What do you think his friends thought of his behaviour?

Reproduced with permission from *Bible Storybags*® published by BRF 2011 (978 0 85746 073 8) www.barnabasinschools.org.uk

THE BOX (THE TREASURE IN THE FIELD)

The rocky road

The prodigal son

Using the storybag® in Assembly

Before the assembly, print some award certificates and ask staff to suggest people who deserve awards for different types of behaviour, such as courage, persistence, caring and so on. Show clips of award ceremonies or talk about them and do a short role-play with another member of staff or older pupil. Talk about the people who get public awards. Give out the awards in the assembly. Explain that admitting you were wrong is not often recognized as deserving an award, but it requires great courage. Introduce the Bible story (see Introduction, page 7).

Present the story using the storybag® or the web version (see pages 75–79) and the biblical material (see page 73).

> **Comment**
> This story is a parable told by Jesus to describe what God is like. Jesus taught that God cared for everyone. He painted word-pictures of God that depicted him as a loving father. The elder brother stands for the religious authorities, some of whom thought that God would not want to accept people who had done wrong.

Reflection

Look at the painting *The Return of the Prodigal Son* by Rembrandt (available on the website www.biblical-art.com > biblical subject > New Testament > Gospels, Jesus, public ministry: words of Jesus > parables. Use the painting as a basis for reflection.

✪ Look at the father—the suffering in his face, his bent body.
✪ Look at the son—his torn clothes, his worn shoes, his head resting on the father.
✪ Look at the father's hands—holding, comforting.
✪ Look at the other figures—looking on, judging.

 Prayer (optional)
Demonstrate breaking wool and cotton. Read the following:

Cotton can break,
Wool can snap,
But the love of God is an invisible thread that can never be broken.

Read the following extract from Romans 8:35–39 (adapted)

Nothing can separate us from the love of God:
Not trouble or suffering,
Not death or danger,
Nothing in earth,
Nothing in heaven,
Nothing in the present,
Nothing in the future.
Nothing in all creation can ever separate us from the love of God.

Dear God, we thank you that you are like a loving father who is always waiting and watching, ready to accept people no matter what they have done.

Using the storybag® in RE

Introduce the subject using some of the material from the assembly introduction (see page 72).

Select the appropriate script and turn to pages 9 and 10 to find ways of using it.

Biblical material

Luke 15:11–32

There was once a man who had two sons. The younger son was bored with being at home so he asked his father for his share of the family money. The younger son took all his money and left home for a far country, and there he spent all his money on parties and wild living. Soon his money ran out and food became so short in that country that the boy was forced to get a job feeding pigs to survive. He became so hungry that he wanted to eat the pigs' food.

After a while he came to his senses, and he said to himself, 'Even my father's servants are better fed than this! I will go home and I will ask Dad to take me back as a servant. I know I don't deserve to be treated as his son any more.' The son started the long journey home but, while he was still some way off, his father spotted him, for he had been watching and waiting for him. The father ran to the boy and hugged him. The boy began his speech, asking his father to take him back as a servant, but his father would have none of it. Instead he accepted him back as a son and threw a party for him.

Meanwhile, the elder brother heard the noise of the party and became cross. Why should his brother be accepted back after wasting all that money? He refused to join the party, so he stayed outside. The father came out and talked to him. He listened to the elder brother's complaints and said, 'Everything I have is yours, but for now let us celebrate, for the son that I thought was lost is found. I thought he was dead but he is alive.'

> **Note:** For a comment on this story, see the assembly section (page 72).

Follow-up activities

(See also pages 11 and 12.) Select from these activities according to the age and aptitude of your pupils.

1. Create a display of this story. Make the background by using patterned paper. Add two-dimensional versions of items from the story, except the rocks, which can be made from screwed-up tissue paper and stapled to the display. Add questions and pupil comments. Older pupils can run a long thread horizontally along the bottom of the display. Hang pieces of paper from the thread, and on the pieces of paper write the invisible things that connect us to other people or God, such as love, loyalty, need and so on.

2. Explore how artists express their understanding of this story, and encourage pupils to do the same. What moment in the story would they choose to paint? Why? The websites listed below are active at the time of writing.

- www.Jesusmafa.com > mini posters
- www.mccrimmons.com > search 'Jesus our hope'
- www.biblical-art.com > biblical subject > New Testament > Gospels, Jesus, public ministry: words of Jesus > parables
- www.biblepicturegallery.com

3. Imagine you are in an editor's office. He or she is putting together a book for Christians, and you have to persuade the editor to include this story in the book that is being published. What arguments will you use to persuade the editor that it is an important story?

4. Create thought bubbles for the son. Use different colours for going and returning. Create thought bubbles for the father for different moments in the story. Do the thoughts change? If so, what causes the change? Do some thoughts or feelings stay the same? Why?

5. Create tableaux of different moments in the story, which can be photographed and captioned. Pay careful attention to body language, gesture and expression. The photographs can be put together to create a photo story of the parable. Which is the most significant scene? Why?

6. Write the letter that the son might have written to his father when he wanted to come home. Think about times when you have said 'sorry'. How did you express it? What sort of courage does it take to say 'sorry'?

Symbols used in this story

● The road: life's journey. The road is harder on the way back as it is difficult to admit we have been wrong.
● The rocks: the hard things we have to do, the things that cause us to stumble or fall in life, difficulties or temptations we face.
● The invisible thread: the bond of love between God and people.
● Torn heart: the pain of love rejected.
● Coins: in this context, they represent independence.

Reflective activity

Sitting in a circle, ask children to hold their hands in front of them and grasp a length of wool tied to make a circle. The wool can be fed through the hands so that it *slowly* moves. As they feel it moving, ask pupils to think about the invisible things that bind us together (just as love bound the father to the son in the story).

Assessment

Assess the pupils' understanding by observing them replaying the script, or ask them to talk about the display or write about it.

Background information and understanding the story

This is a story about love, forgiveness, acceptance and the fatherhood of God. The boy did not deserve to be taken back: it was mercy rather than justice that he was given. He got more than he deserved.

The story is a parable told by Jesus to describe what God is like. It is one of three parables about things that are lost. The other two are the lost coin and the lost sheep (Luke 15:1–11: see page 44).

The majority of people in this time and place were farmers, and sons would have followed their fathers in working the land.

The elder son would have inherited two-thirds and the younger son one-third of the family's wealth. The elder son's inheritance would not have been altered: his inheritance was protected. The elder brother in the story represents the religious authorities of the day, who were scandalized by Jesus' ministry to people they called 'outcasts and sinners'. The authorities were so occupied with being 'right' that they could not rejoice when someone else changed for the better.

Working with pigs would have been the worst job a Jewish boy could do, as they are seen as unclean animals for people of the Jewish faith.

Useful websites

The websites listed below are active at the time of writing.

● www.request.org.uk (browse teacher's area)
● www.textweek.com/art/art.htm > Jacob to Mustard Seed > Jesus/Christ > Parables

Script 1

Unpacking the bag

My bag is richly patterned, for this is the pattern of life.
There is a road in my bag, rocky and rough.
There are rocks in my bag that make the road hard to walk on.
There are people in my bag—a son and a loving father.
There is money in my bag that is soon gone.
There are tears in my bag that fall like rain.
There are things for a party, for someone is celebrating.

The story

Our story takes place on a patterned cloth, for this is a story about life, and life is richly patterned *(place bag and smooth)*. Across the cloth runs a road and the road is dotted with rocks *(place road and rocks)*. At one end stands a father who is sad *(place father)*, for his son has left home and he worries about him *(drop tears)*. At the other end of the road is his son *(place son)*. He is happy to be going to a new place and he has money to spend *(drop money on the cloth)*. Soon the money runs out and the son is hungry and lonely *(sweep away money)*.

The father still stands at the end of the road, watching and waiting, hoping his son is all right *(lift father and replace)*.

The son becomes so hungry *(rub stomach)* that he decides to return home, so he starts the journey back *(start the journey home)*. The road is long and hard and on the way he thinks of all that has happened *(move the son along the road, bumping into rocks, resting and so on)*. He thinks of how he has wasted his father's money *(lift and drop money again)*. He thinks about how he has hurt his father's feelings *(drop tears)*. He knows that he does not deserve to be forgiven *(shake head)*.

As soon as the father sees the son, he runs to him *(move son and father together to embrace)*. All the past is forgiven. All the wrongs are wiped out. The father throws a party to celebrate his son's return *(throw streamers)*.

You will need
- A patterned bag
- 2 'people'
- A dull brown ribbon
- Screwed-up brown paper for rocks
- Toy coins
- Silver paper tear shapes
- Safe party items (e.g. streamers)

Questions
(See also page 11.)

- Why does the father keep watching?
- What makes the son return?
- What do you think about the son's behaviour?

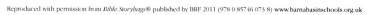

Reproduced with permission from *Bible Storybags®* published by BRF 2011 (978 0 85746 073 8) www.barnabasinschools.org.uk

THE ROCKY ROAD (THE PRODIGAL SON)

Script 2

You will need

- ❖ A patterned bag
- ❖ 2 'people'
- ❖ A dull brown ribbon
- ❖ Screwed-up brown paper for rocks
- ❖ Toy coins
- ❖ Silver paper tear shapes
- ❖ Safe party items (e.g. streamers)
- ❖ Imaginary thread (just hold your finger and thumb together as if something is there)
- ❖ A paper heart shape

● Unpacking the bag

My bag is richly patterned, for this is the pattern of life.
There is a road in my bag, rocky and rough.
There are rocks in my bag that make people stumble.
There are people in my bag—a bored son and a loving father.
There is an invisible thread in my bag that binds them together.
There is gold in my bag that is soon gone.
There is a heart in my bag that will be broken.

● The story

Our story takes place on a patterned cloth.	*Hold up bag*
The pattern is rich and complicated...	*Run finger round the patterns*
for this is the pattern of life...	*Place and smooth bag*
and life is rarely simple.	
Across the cloth runs a road...	*Place road*
the rocky road to 'freedom'...	*Add rocks by road*
the road to repentance, the road to forgiveness.	
Down the road walks a boy.	*Place boy on road*
His pockets are heavy with coins...	*Drop coins on the bag*
his heart is light with hopes. He walks the road of freedom.	*Move boy down the road a little*
He does not notice the rocks...	*Avoid rocks*
he does not look back.	*Stand boy still, shake your head*

Reproduced with permission from *Bible Storybags®* published by BRF 2011 (978 0 85746 073 8) www.barnabasinschools.org.uk

THE ROCKY ROAD (THE PRODIGAL SON)

Watching the boy is the father.	*Place father watching boy*
His heart is torn with sorrow…	*Show heart, then tear in two*
his eyes drop tears…	*Scatter tears*
he fears for the boy with the coins and the hopes.	*Indicate boy and coins*
He watches his son walk…	*Move boy a little on the road, avoiding rocks*
the rocky road of freedom.	
This is the invisible thread…	*Hold up imaginary thread*
that joins them. It stretches from the father to the son.	*Indicate thread joining them*
It cannot be broken.	*Shake head*
The father watches the boy disappear…	*Lift father*
but still he does not move.	*Shake head*
He continues to watch the road…	*Indicate road*
he continues to hold the thread…	*Hold up imaginary thread*
the thread that cannot be broken.	
The boy does not notice the thread…	*Shake head*
that joins him to his father. He does not feel it pulling at him.	*Pull imaginary thread*
He travels on, ignoring the rocks, ignoring the thread.	*Move boy to end of road*
He is free.	
Arriving at a far country…	*Scatter coins on cloth*
the boy spends his money and soon both hopes and gold are gone.	*Pick up coins and remove them*

Reproduced with permission from *Bible Storybags®* published by BRF 2011 (978 0 85746 073 8) www.barnabasinschools.org.uk

THE ROCKY ROAD (THE PRODIGAL SON)

Still he ignores the thread, the thread that cannot be broken.	*Hold up invisible thread*
The boy is lonely and poor.	*Indicate boy*
No friends…	*Shake head*
no money…	*Open hands, palm up*
no hope.	*Shake head*
Still the father watches…	*Lift father*
watches and waits, pulling on the thread that joins them.	*Pull imaginary thread*
The boy sinks into despair, but in his sadness he feels the pull of the thread.	*Pull thread*
He knows his father is watching and waiting…	*Lift father*
but he cannot go back. He has caused too much trouble…	*Shake head*
done too much wrong.	
Still the father watches…	*Indicate or lift father*
watches and waits, pulling on the thread that joins them…	*Pull imaginary thread*
like a rescuer hauling in a drowning man.	
Finally the son decides to return.	*Turn son to face father*
As he stumbles along the road…	*Move along road*
the rocky road to repentance, he goes over his failures…	*Bump against rocks*
he rehearses his wrongs. The road seems longer than he remembered.	*Indicate length of road*

Reproduced with permission from *Bible Storybags*® published by BRF 2011 (978 0 85746 073 8) www.barnabasinschools.org.uk

THE ROCKY ROAD (THE PRODIGAL SON)

It is strewn with rocks he never noticed before.   *Lift rocks*

The way is hard.

Still the father watches…   *Lift father*

watches and waits,
pulling hard on the thread that joins them…   *Pull thread hard*

for his son needs him.
He sees him in the distance,
stumbling along the road…   *Touch road*

the road that leads to forgiveness.

The father runs to his son.
The son collapses into his father's arms.   *Place figures together*

The thread lies loose at their feet…   *Indicate imaginary thread*

the thread that can never be broken.

Questions
(See also page 11.)

- What is the thread? Why can't it be broken?
- Why does the road have more than one name?
- What makes the son return?
- What keeps the father watching?

Reproduced with permission from *Bible Storybags*® published by BRF 2011 (978 0 85746 073 8) www.barnabasinschools.org.uk

THE ROCKY ROAD (THE PRODIGAL SON)

The whirlwind and the calm

Martha and Mary

●●●

Using the storybag® in Assembly

To introduce the subject, play busy music and talk about all the things you have to do today. Create a giant list of things to do. End by saying that you need to keep calm and not panic. Play some quiet music and talk about needing time to think and be quiet and calm, because it helps you cope with the busy times. Today's story is about two very different people—one who was always busy and one who was quiet and calm. Introduce the Bible story (see Introduction, page 7).

Present the story using the storybag® or the web version (see pages 83–86) and the biblical material (see page 81).

Comment

In this story, Jesus is not saying that it is OK to let one person do all the work. He is saying that there is a time for work and a time just to be with people. On this occasion Mary got it right. If he was only there for a few hours, it was not appropriate to spend all the time in the kitchen. Jesus calms Martha without criticism, recognizing that she was acting from the best of motives. His kindness kills the anger.

Christians believe that it is right to do things for God—to help people and to work for justice in the world. They also take time just to be with God as a friend, to talk and listen to him. Work for God also has to be done in the right attitude. Helping others should be done willingly, not in an attitude of bitterness or self-pity.

Reflection

Play busy music and ask pupils to think of times when it is appropriate to be busy. Play calm music and ask pupils to think of times when it is appropriate to be quiet.

Prayer *(optional)*

There are different times in life: there is a time to be busy, and a time to be still. There is a time for working and a time for resting. There is a time for talking and a time for listening. Help us, God, to know the right time for each.

Introduce the subject using some of the material from the assembly introduction (see page 80).

Select the appropriate script and turn to pages 9 and 10 to find ways of using it.

Biblical material

Luke 10:38–42

One day, Jesus came to a village called Bethany and decided to call in on some friends called Martha and Mary. He often stopped at their house if he wanted to rest. Both sisters were delighted to see him, but they reacted very differently to his coming: Martha went on working to get dinner ready but Mary stopped and sat down to listen to him.

The more Martha worked, the more bitter and angry she got. She felt sorry for herself. Why should she have to work alone? Why wasn't Mary helping? It wasn't fair! Finally, Martha felt so sorry for herself that she went into the room where Jesus was sitting and all her anger burst out. 'Lord, don't you care that Mary has left me with all the work? It's not fair that I should do everything by myself!'

Jesus looked up at Martha and said gently, 'Martha, I can see that you are worried and upset about all the work, but I want your company and friendship more than your cooking. Mary has done what is right: she stopped work and came and talked with me when I arrived. I am only here for a few hours. We can eat something simple, so take off your apron and come and sit down.'

Martha did as he said and the two sisters were able to enjoy his company.

> **Note:** For a comment on this story, see the assembly section (page 80).

Follow-up activities

(See also pages 11 and 12.) Select from these activities according to the age and aptitude of your pupils.

1. Create a display of the script using patterned and plain backgrounds. Add two-dimensional versions of the items from the story—except for the weed, which can be made from screwed-up tissue and stapled to the display. Add questions and pupil comments, thought and speech bubbles, and Blake's poem 'The poison tree':

I was angry with my friend:
I told my wrath, my wrath did end.
I was angry with my foe;
I told it not, my wrath did grow.

And I water'd it in fears,
Night and morning with my tears;
And I sunned it with my smiles
And with soft deceitful wiles.

And it grew both day and night,
Till it bore an apple bright;
And my foe beheld it shine,
And he knew that it was mine,

And into my garden stole
When the night had veil'd the pole:
In the morning glad I see
My foe outstretch'd beneath the tree.
William Blake (d. 1827)

2. Create a diagram of this story with pictures and captions. Use colours on clothes or backgrounds to indicate the mood of each picture.

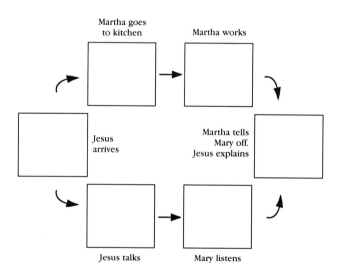

If you met Martha or Mary, what would you want to say to her? Write what you would say in a speech bubble.

3. Think about yourself: are you more of a Mary or more of a Martha? Are you a 'doer' or do you like to stop and think and reflect? Are you a mixture of both? Mark your response on the line, according to who you are most like. Interview some friends who are happy to mark their responses. Think of a way of showing your results.

Martha --- **Mary**

4. Encourage pupils to listen to music as they reflect on the story. They can express their own ideas and understanding through sound or music. Some suggested pieces are as follows.

Busy music

- 'Song of the Spirit' from *Adiemus II: Cantata Mundi* by K. Jenkins
- 'The flight of the bumble bee' by Rimskij-Korsakov

Calm music

- 'Serenade No 13 in G Major' from *Eine Kleine Nachtmusik* by Mozart
- *Piano Sonata No 14 in C Sharp Minor* by Beethoven

5. Explore how artists express their understanding of this story, and encourage pupils to do the same. The websites listed below are active at the time of writing.

- www.Jesusmafa.com > mini posters
- www.nationalgallery.org.uk > search 'Martha and Mary'
- www.biblical-art.com > biblical subject > New Testament > Gospels, Jesus, public ministry: encounters
- www.biblepicturegallery.com
- www.heqigallery.com (browse galleries)

6. With older pupils, read Blake's poem 'The poison tree' (see page 81). Discuss how disagreements can grow out of proportion if we 'water' them with bitterness, resentment and self-pity. Create droplets in which the pupils write the things that 'water' a difficult situation and make it grow. The droplets can be added to the display.

Symbols used in this story

- Weeds: bitterness that is allowed to grow.
- Whirlwind: overactivity.
- Patterned cloth: busyness of life.
- Pale blue cloth: calm.

Reflective activity

With older pupils, create a reflective corner with a busy patterned cloth and a calm coloured cloth. Have squares of green tissue available in a basket so that pupils can create 'weeds'. Place the containers from the bag on the cloth (a tray can be provided for this activity), display William Blake's poem, and add a small waste paper basket. Display a card that reads:

As you make your 'weed' and place it on the tray, think of a time when you have felt like Martha. Sprinkle over a little 'bitterness' and 'self-pity'. Think of one way of overcoming bitterness and self-pity. Sometimes words of kindness help, at other times there might be an injustice to put right. Squash the weed and place it in the waste paper basket.

With younger pupils, make a reflective corner by covering a small table with a cloth and display the bag for the pupils to replay the story. Have music to play and place a few questions: for example, 'Have you ever felt like Martha?'

Assessment

Assess the pupils' understanding by observing them replaying the script, or ask them to talk about the display or write about it.

Background information and understanding the story

Martha and Mary had a brother called Lazarus who was also a friend of Jesus. Their home in Bethany was the nearest Jesus had to a home in the south of the country. His family home was in Nazareth in the north.

Women were not usually taught to read and were considered of low status. Throughout his ministry, however, Jesus treated women with respect. The fact that Mary stopped and listened shows that Jesus treated her as someone worthy of teaching.

Food had to be prepared from scratch. Jesus recognized Martha's work, but put emphasis on the relationship rather than the food.

Useful websites

The websites listed below are active at the time of writing.

- www.Jesusmafa.com > mini posters
- www.nationalgallery.org.uk > search 'Martha and Mary'
- www.biblical-art.com > biblical subject > New Testament> Gospels, Jesus, public ministry: encounters
- www.biblepicturegallery.com
- www.heqigallery.com (browse galleries)

Script 1

Unpacking the bag

My bag is brightly coloured with a busy pattern, for this is a story of busyness and work.
My bag is soft and blue, for this is a story of calm.
There are two sisters in my bag who are very different.
One is always busy: she works like a whirlwind.
One is quiet and calm.
There is a friend in my bag who speaks words of kindness.

The story

Our story takes place on a busy cloth, for there is much work to be done and life is busy *(show patterned side of bag)*. Our story takes place on a soft, blue cloth *(show blue side)*, for this is also a story of quiet and calm. Our story starts with two sisters waiting *(place cloth with busy side showing)* and, while they wait, there is much work to be done *(place sisters on cloth)*. There is washing and sweeping, cooking and dusting *(move women around)*. The house is a whirlwind of work: the women are never still.

Then the friend arrives and everything stops *(flip over a section of the bag so that blue shows; place Jesus on the blue)*. For a moment, all is calm and quiet *(place sisters with Jesus)*. Then one sister remembers that all is not finished, and off she goes to cook and clean again *(move one sister to busy side of bag)*. While one works *(lift busy sister)*, the other listens to the friend *(lift calm sister)*.

Anger grows inside the busy sister as she works *(point inside yourself)*. Why should she work alone? Why should she do it all? *(lift busy sister)*. Upset and angry, she tells her sister so *(move busy sister next to calm one)*. Then the friend speaks words of kindness *(lift Jesus)* and the anger dies. The friend calls her to sit and rest. All is calm again and the house is a place of peace *(place all on the blue cloth)*.

You will need
- A bag with a busy pattern on one side and pale blue on the other
- 3 'people': 2 sisters and Jesus

Questions
(See also page 11.)

- How do the sisters differ?
- Why is one woman angry?
- What gets rid of anger?

Reproduced with permission from *Bible Storybags*® published by BRF 2011 (978 0 85746 073 8) www.barnabasinschools.org.uk

THE WHIRLWIND AND THE CALM (MARTHA AND MARY)

Script 2

● Unpacking the bag

You will need

❖ A bag with a busy pattern on one side and pale blue on the other
❖ 3 'people': 2 sisters and Jesus
❖ A paper heart
❖ A ribbon stick (crêpe paper streamers on a folded art straw) for the whirlwind
❖ A weed (green tissue paper)
❖ 2 plastic pots, one labelled 'self-pity' containing chopped yellow paper, the other labelled 'bitterness' containing chopped brown paper

My bag is patterned, busy and bright...
My bag is pale blue, the colour of silence (show reverse of bag).
There are people in my bag:
two sisters and a friend who comes to visit.
There is a whirlwind of work in my bag (whirl the streamers)
and a place of peace and calm (stop streamers with other hand).
There is a weed in my bag, a weed of anger,
fed and watered by self-pity and bitterness.

● The story

Our story takes place on a soft blue cloth...	*Show blue side of bag*
the colour of silence. Our story also takes place on a patterned cloth.	*Hold up patterned side.* *Place bag patterned side up*
The cloth is covered in a busy pattern, for life can be full of activity.	
There are two sisters who are very different.	*Show two sisters*
One is a whirlwind of activity...	*Place one sister on cloth*
one is quiet and calm...	*Place other sister on cloth*
But today, both are busy getting ready for their friend.	
Before he comes, they cook and clean...	*Move sisters about*
they dust and sweep. Then the friend comes...	*Flip over a section of bag so that blue shows.* *Place Jesus on the blue*
and everything stops. The two sisters greet him.	*Move sisters to blue section*

Reproduced with permission from *Bible Storybags*® published by BRF 2011 (978 0 85746 073 8) www.barnabasinschools.org.uk

THE WHIRLWIND AND THE CALM (MARTHA AND MARY)

All is quiet and calm. Then one continues with her whirlwind of work.	*Move busy sister to patterned section. Spin streamers*
The other sister sits and is quiet.	*Use other hand to stop steamers*
One is busy and active...	*Lift one sister*
one is calm and listens.	*Lift the other sister*
Both wish to serve their friend.	*Lift the man*
In the busy whirl of work...	*Whirl streamers, then stop*
one sister spins.	*Indicate busy sister*
Her head aches...	*Touch head*
her feet hurt...	*Indicate your feet*
her hands are never still...	*Move hands*
for she wants to serve her friend.	*Lift the man*
In the quiet, the other sister sits.	*Lift calm sister*
Her mind thinks on his words...	*Touch head*
her heart ponders his teaching ...	*Touch heart*
and her hands are still... for she, too, wishes to serve her friend.	*Lift man*
In the busy kitchen, anger grows inside one sister like a weed.	*Place weed*
It is fed by self-pity...	*Scatter tissue from 'self-pity' pot*
it is watered with bitterness...	*Scatter tissue from 'bitterness' pot*
it leads to angry words.	

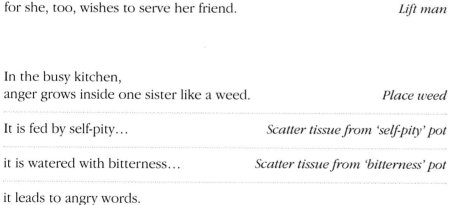

Reproduced with permission from *Bible Storybags®* published by BRF 2011 (978 0 85746 073 8) www.barnabasinschools.org.uk

THE WHIRLWIND AND THE CALM (MARTHA AND MARY)

Then he speaks her name, And words of kindness kill the weed.	*Crush weed with your fist*
In the quiet, both sisters rest in his care.	*Place all three together on blue cloth*
Life can be a whirlwind…	*Spin streamers*
life can be quiet.	*Stop streamers with other hand*
We can serve in the whirlwind…	*Spin streamers*
we can serve in the quiet.	*Stop streamers with other hand*
We can serve in different ways, but never with bitterness…	*Scatter tissue from 'bitterness' pot*
never with self-pity…	*Scatter tissue from 'self-pity' pot*
only with love.	*Show heart*

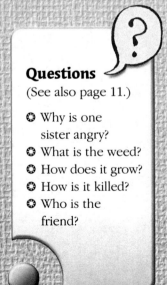

Questions
(See also page 11.)

- Why is one sister angry?
- What is the weed?
- How does it grow?
- How is it killed?
- Who is the friend?

Reproduced with permission from *Bible Storybags*® published by BRF 2011 (978 0 85746 073 8) www.barnabasinschools.org.uk

THE WHIRLWIND AND THE CALM (MARTHA AND MARY)

The hands

The healing of the man with leprosy

To introduce the subject, talk about different things we can do with our hands (write, clap, catch a ball) and ask pupils to demonstrate. Have a range of activities that pupils can join in with (a few at a time) to show how they can use their hands. Talk about times when we are poorly and about the people who help us. People can use their hands to comfort, help and heal.

There is an illness that can affect hands (and other parts of the body). It causes body parts to lose their feeling, so that they become damaged. The disease is called leprosy. If a person with leprosy put their hands in the fire, they would not feel it and their hands would be burnt. (Reassure the children that leprosy is now curable and is not present in Europe.) In Jesus' time, leprosy was not curable and people were afraid of catching it. Introduce the Bible story (see Introduction, page 7).

Present the story using the storybag® or the web version (see pages 90–92) and the biblical material (see page 88).

Comment

This is a story about healing. It shows Jesus' compassion (love) for the rejected people of society, the people that no one else wanted to know. The person was not only healed in body; his feelings were healed too, as he was no longer on his own. Some versions of the Bible say that Jesus was angry—not angry with the man, but angry that people suffered in this way.

Reflection

Ask pupils to look at their hands while you read the following:

Hands can do many things:
they can make and destroy,
play and bully,
hurt or heal.
Hands do not act by themselves.
We decide what they do.

Prayer *(optional)*

Thank you, heavenly Father, for hands that we can use for good in the world. Help us to use our hands creatively and well, making our world a better place.

Introduce the subject using some of the material from the assembly introduction (see page 87).

Select the appropriate script and turn to pages 9 and 10 to find ways of using it.

Biblical material

Mark 1:40–44; Matthew 8:1–4; Luke 5:12–15 (see also Luke 17:11–19)

One day, as Jesus was walking along, a man with leprosy came up to him and knelt before him. 'Lord, if you want to, you could heal me,' he said. Jesus was filled with compassion for this lonely man who suffered with this terrible disease. 'Of course I want to,' said Jesus. 'Be healed!' Immediately the man was healed, and Jesus told him to go to the priest and show him that he was cured so that people would no longer be afraid to come near him.

> **Note:** For a comment on this story, see the assembly section (page 87).

Follow-up activities

(See also pages 11 and 12.) Select from these activities according to the age and aptitude of your pupils.

1. Create a Big Book of the story as a class, making sure that you communicate the meaning. Add images and some of the script on each page or use the words (suitably adapted) of the Bible story. Assess the book: have you communicated the message of the story?

2. Design a 'thank you' card from the man who was healed. Discuss when we say 'thank you' and why. Learn the sign language for 'thank you'. Pupils can create their own sign to express the meaning of the phrase (see www.britishsignlanguage.com).

3. Encourage pupils to listen to music as they reflect on the story. They can express their own ideas or understanding through sound or music. Suggested pieces are as follows.

- Anger: 'Ride of the Valkyries' by Wagner
- Love and compassion: 'What a wonderful world' by L. Armstrong
- Loneliness: Opening to the *William Tell* overture by Rossini; 'Largo' from *Symphony No 9* by Dvorak
- Joy: 'Ode to joy' from *Symphony No 9* by Beethoven; *Capriccio Italienne* by Tchaikovsky (joyful second section)

4. Using the music, create a dance based on the script. Explore the following:

- Togetherness and separation
- Loneliness and encounter
- Love, anger and healing

Photograph parts of the dance and add them to the display.

5. Create a display by covering a board with dark red paper and adding two-dimensional versions of the items from the bag. Add questions and comments from the pupils. Sections of the script could act as captions. Put a 'hands' border around the display.

6. Explore how artists express their understanding of this story, and encourage pupils to do the same. What advice would they give an artist to help him or her capture the significance of the story? The websites listed below are active at the time of writing.

- www.biblepicturegallery.com
- www.Jesusmafa.com > mini posters
- www.biblical-art.com > biblical subject > New Testament > Gospels, Jesus, public ministry: miracles

Symbols used in this story

- Hands: help, asking, caring.
- Touch: compassion.
- Dark red: pain, loneliness and anger.

Reflective activity

Have a plastic tray filled with dry play-sand, and an attractive basket of hand shapes cut from card of different colours. Encourage pupils to think of things that they take for granted, that they might say 'thank you' for. Whom would they thank (parents, meal supervisors, teachers, God and so on)? Invite them, if they wish, to write the name of a person they want to thank on the back of a hand shape, or draw the person. The hand shapes can be stuck in the sand so that it looks like a 'sea' of waving hands.

Assessment

Assess the pupils' understanding by observing them replaying the script, or ask them to talk about the display or write about it.

Background information and understanding the story

Throughout the Gospels, Jesus is seen to heal people from things that hurt the mind, body and spirit. Jesus was not just a teacher: his teaching was linked to his healing. He spoke of the love of God for all, then he touched people who had leprosy.

Christians are divided concerning miracles: some believe in them and believe that they still happen; others do not. Some Christians understand miracles symbolically; others accept them as events that happened.

Jesus often told people to keep quiet about the miracles they witnessed. Otherwise, in an age before modern medicine, he would have been swamped by people seeking physical healing, allowing him no time to teach and be with people.

People thought that leprosy (Hansen's disease) was very infectious, but we now know that it is quite difficult to catch. The regulations in force at the time meant that anyone diagnosed with such a disease had to leave their family and live alone. Sometimes groups of people lived together, as in the case of the ten men with leprosy (Luke 17:11–19). Leprosy is now curable, but there is no vaccination against it.

The priests certified that a person was clear of the disease and able to return to the community. As their word carried weight, this helped people to integrate without being suspected by others of spreading disease.

Useful websites

The websites listed below are active at the time of writing.

- ✪ www.theway2go.org > the hub > yellow ball> the leper
- ✪ www.leprosymission.org
- ✪ www.textweek.com/art/art.htm > Jacob to Mustard Seed > Jesus/Christ > Healing

You will need

❖ A dark red bag
❖ 4 'people':
   1 man, 1 woman,
   1 child and Jesus
❖ Toy houses
❖ Paper tear shapes

Questions
(See also page 11.)

✪ Why is the man away from his family?
✪ Why is the man who heals him not afraid?
✪ What sort of strength does this person have?

Script 1

Unpacking the bag

*My bag is dark red and in my bag there is a family—
a man, his wife and their child.
There is a house in my bag, where people live.
In my bag is a man, strong in love and power.*

The story

Our story takes place on a dark red cloth *(place cloth and smooth)*, for this is a story of pain and loneliness. It starts with a family—a mum, a dad and a child *(place three figures on the cloth with the man in the centre)*. The family live together in a small village *(place houses)*. All is well until, one day, the man becomes ill with a disease that other people can catch. He cannot stay with his wife and child, for they might catch his illness, so he goes away on his own *(move man away from his family, leaving a gap)*. The family are sad *(place tears)*. The man is sad and lonely *(place more tears)*. The illness becomes worse and the man's hands become damaged. Soon, he knows, the illness will spread to his whole body.

One day, someone comes walking through the lonely place *(place Jesus on cloth)*. He is not scared of the illness *(shake head)*. He is not frightened of the disease *(shake head)*. His love and power are strong *(walk Jesus near to the man)*. He holds out his hand and touches the man who is ill *(hands touch)*. The illness is defeated and the man is well again—his hands are whole *(hold out your hands)*. The family are together again *(place man in the gap between mother and child)* and the man who healed him goes on his quiet way *(walk Jesus off bag)*.

Reproduced with permission from *Bible Storybags®* published by BRF 2011 (978 0 85746 073 8) www.barnabasinschools.org.uk

THE HANDS (THE HEALING OF THE MAN WITH LEPROSY)

Script 2

Unpacking the bag

My bag is red, for this is a story of pain and anger.
There are tears in my bag, for this is a story of loneliness.
There is a man in my bag, all alone.
There is a family in the bag who miss the man.
There is a village in my bag, where the family live.
There is someone in the bag who feels for the man in his pain and
loneliness.

You will need
- A dark red bag
- 4 'people':
  1 man, 1 woman,
  1 child and Jesus
- Toy houses
- Paper tear shapes

The story

Our story takes place on a deep red cloth…	*Place bag and smooth*
for this is a story of pain. It starts with a man…	*Place man*
who has a wife…	*Place wife on one side*
and a child…	*Place child on the other*
a man who has a house in a village.	*Place houses*
But now he is ill and he has to leave them all to live in a lonely place.	*Move man away*
He goes far from his home and family. He longs to see his wife and child…	*Place tears*
but he cannot, for he loves them.	
Our story ends with someone…	*Place Jesus on cloth*
who goes walking in the lonely place…	*Slowly walk him to the man*
someone who sees the pain. Inside, his heart burns…	*Indicate your heart*
and his anger roars against it.	

THE HANDS (THE HEALING OF THE MAN WITH LEPROSY)

Older pupils

This is the story of hands...	*Hold up your right hand, palm facing pupils*
stretched out in healing.	*Stretch out right hand*
This is the story of hands...	*Hold up left hand, palm facing pupils*
damaged by illness...	*Slowly curl fingers inwards*
but stretched out in hope.	*Stretch hand, still curled*
In a moment, the hands meet.	*The two hands meet*
Illness meets healing...	*Uncurl left hand*
and disease is destroyed. Now there is hope.	*Show both hands open, palm up*
Life begins again.	*Move man to child and wife*
The hands that, for years...	*Show hands*
have never felt a touch...	*Hug yourself*
hugged a family. Hands hold, hands pray...	*Lace hands in prayer*
and a heart says 'Thank you.'	*Sign language 'Thank you'*

Questions
(See also page 11.)

- Who is the person who heals the man?
- Why is he angry?
- What do you think is wrong with the man who is unwell?
- Why does he stay alone out of love for his family?

Reproduced with permission from *Bible Storybags*® published by BRF 2011 (978 0 85746 073 8) www.barnabasinschools.org.uk

THE HANDS (THE HEALING OF THE MAN WITH LEPROSY)

The monster

The storm on the lake

 Using the storybag® in Assembly

To introduce the subject, talk about people who help us when we are afraid. With younger children, use a picture book that explores the theme of fear and how to overcome it. Discuss storms and allay any fears concerning thunderstorms. For older pupils, go to www.perfectstorm.net for images of storms. Explain that today's story is about a storm on a lake, which frightened people. Introduce the Bible story (see Introduction, page 7).

Present the story using the storybag® or the web version (see pages 96–99) and the biblical material (see page 94).

Comment

For Christians, this story shows Jesus' compassion (love) and his power. Jesus uses his power for the good of other people. Jesus did not calm every storm: there must have been others. Christians do not believe that he removes every difficulty in life, but he did promise to be with people, just as he was with the disciples in the boat. When life gets 'stormy'—when difficulties and troubles come—Christians believe that Jesus is always there as an invisible friend who helps. Christians believe that people never have to face anything alone.

Reflection

Ask pupils to think about what they have heard while you play some short extracts of music (see suggestions on page 94). End with the calm music and do a calming exercise, such as stilling each part of the body in turn.

 ### Prayer *(optional)*

Thank you, Jesus, that you are always there, in good times and in bad. Help us when we are afraid.

Using the storybag® in RE

Introduce the subject using some of the material from the assembly introduction (see page 93).

Select the appropriate script and turn to pages 9 and 10 to find ways of using it.

Biblical material

Matthew 8:23–27; Mark 4:35–41; Luke 8:22–25

Jesus had been busy all day, teaching and healing people, and now he was very, very tired. At the end of the day he got into a boat, and his friends, the disciples, started to row the boat to the other side of the lake (called the Sea of Galilee). While they rowed, Jesus slept in the back of the boat.

Without warning, a terrible storm hit the lake and the waves began to come over the side. Jesus was so tired that even the noise of the storm did not wake him. Several of the disciples were fishermen and they were used to the storms that often hit the lake, but this was different. They struggled with the oars but it was no use—they could not make the shore. They knew they were in great danger.

In desperation, the disciples woke Jesus up. 'Master, Master, don't you care that we are drowning?' Jesus got up and replied, 'Why are you afraid?' Then he stood up and said to the storm, 'Peace! Be quiet!' The wind and rain stopped and it was completely calm.

The disciples were amazed. 'Who is this man?' they said. 'Even the winds and the waves obey him!'

> **Note:** For a comment on this story, see the assembly section (page 93).

Follow-up activities

(See also pages 11 and 12.) Select from these activities according to the age and aptitude of your pupils.

1. Create a display of this story on a dark blue background, using two-dimensional versions of the items from the bag. Add pupils' comments and questions on storm clouds (see activity 5). As a class, suggest some of the things that make life stormy. (Keep the suggestions impersonal: for example, 'having arguments with friends'.) Some of the suggestions can be written on storm clouds and added to the display.

2. Encourage pupils to listen to music as they reflect on the story. They can express their own ideas and understanding through sound or music:

- Storm and calm afterwards: 'Storm' from *Four Sea Interludes* by Britten
- Storm: *William Tell Overture* (storm section) by Rossini
- Storm: *The Hebrides Overture* (*Fingal's Cave*) by Mendelssohn
- Calm: Pachelbel's *Canon*
- Calm: *L'Arlésienne Suite No 1* (Adagietto) by Bizet

3. Choose one moment in this story and explore it through the senses. What would the people in the boat have tasted, smelt, seen, touched and heard? Pupils could draw symbols to represent each of the five senses. Ask pupils to turn their response into continuous prose. For example, 'The disciples saw the mountainous waves…'.

4. Explore how artists express their understanding of this story, and encourage pupils to do the same. Pupils can paint their own 'storm monster'. For example, the monster's hair might look like a cloud. The websites listed below are active at the time of writing.

- www.jesusmafa.com > mini posters
- www.textweek.com/art/art.htm > Salome to Zechariah > Storms
- www.heqigallery.com (browse galleries)

5. Using a plastic coat hanger, make a mobile of questions to 'hang in the air'. Discuss the story first, then create the questions that pupils would like to ask and display them on storm clouds suspended from the coat hanger. The questions on the mobile can become the focus of discussions.

6. Write a poem about this story, bringing out the storm as a monster, how it was calmed and the reaction afterwards. In the poem, if possible, explore the metaphor of the storm as representing life's troubles (see Psalm 69 for an example).

Symbols used in this story

- The storm: the power of nature and the troubles of life.
- The monster: describing the storm as a monster catches the way it can also stand for fears and troubles. The words Jesus used translate literally as 'Be muzzled', which is an implicit metaphor likening the storm to a monster or animal.
- The sea: Christian life is sometimes described as a sea journey with God as the captain.

Reflective activity

Sail a toy boat in a water tray. As the boat sails, pupils can stir the water to make waves (with supervision). They can think about what helps them when they are afraid. If appropriate, pupils can add prayers to the boat as it sails.

Breton sailors used to pray the prayer, 'O Lord, the sea is so large and my boat is so small' to reflect life as a sea journey. This prayer could be added to a boat.

Assessment

Assess the pupils' understanding by observing them replaying the script, or ask them to talk about the display or write about it.

Background information and understanding the story

Christians understand Jesus' miracles as demonstrations of power and compassion and also as signs pointing to his identity. In this case, he shows that he has the power of the Creator who made the sea (Genesis 1:1–9; Job 38:8–11). Christians believe that Jesus is the Son of God, who was with God from the very beginning, helping to create the world.

Jesus commented once that power went out of him when someone was healed (Luke 8:46). On the occasion of the storm, Jesus had been teaching and healing all day—hence his tiredness.

Christians are divided concerning miracles: some believe in them and believe that they still happen; others do not. Some Christians understand miracles symbolically; others accept them as events that happened.

This story takes place on the Sea of Galilee, which is actually a lake encircled by hills. The wind funnels down the gaps between the hills and hits the lake, causing sudden storms. Fishermen like Peter would have been used to handling boats in a storm on the lake, but this must have been a very wild storm.

Useful websites

The websites listed below are active at the time of writing.

- www.reonline > infants > Bible
- www.request.org.uk (browse teacher's area)
- www.textweek.com/art/art.htm > Salome to Zechariah > Storms

Younger pupils

Questions

(See also page 11.)

✪ Who is the teacher?
✪ Why is he sleeping through the storm?
✪ Why are the friends puzzled?

Script 1

Unpacking the bag

My bag is deep blue, the colour of a stormy sea.
There is a boat in my bag that sails on the water.
There are friends in my bag who sail in the boat.
There is wind in my bag that whips up the sea.
There is thunder in my bag that rocks the earth.
There is lightning in my bag that lights the sky
and a monster storm that endangers the boat.

The story

Our story takes place on a deep blue cloth, for this is the story of a storm at sea *(place bag and smooth)*. On the sea sails a boat *(place boat)*. In the boat are a group of friends *(place four disciples)*. Many of the friends are fishermen; they are used to sailing *(show disciples)*. The teacher is also in the boat *(add Jesus)*. He is tired, very tired. He has been helping people all day, so he sleeps at the back of the boat *(lay down Jesus)*.

Suddenly the wind blows hard and hits the water. The waves rise and the tiny boat is tossed by the sea *(make wind noises and bunch up cloth around boat)*. The friends struggle to control the boat, but the teacher sleeps on *(head on hands to indicate sleep)*. He is so tired, he is not woken by the storm.

The storm gets worse *(make wind noises)*, the thunder rolls *(make thunder noises)* and the lightning cracks *(switch torch on and off)*. It is a monster of a storm. Frightened for their lives, the friends wake the teacher. The teacher stands up *(stand up Jesus)*. 'Peace! Be quiet!' he says to the storm. Suddenly all is calm. The wind ceases *(fade wind noise)*, the thunder stops *(fade thunder noise)* and lightning no longer lights the sky. The waves die down *(smooth the cloth)*.

The friends are amazed. 'Who is this man?' they say. 'He can even stop the wind and the waves.'

Reproduced with permission from *Bible Storybags*® published by BRF 2011 (978 0 85746 073 8) www.barnabasinschools.org.uk

THE MONSTER (THE STORM ON THE LAKE)

Script 2

Unpacking the bag

My bag is dark blue, the blue of an angry sky and an angry sea.
There is rain in my bag that beats and falls.
There is wind in my bag that is wild and wet.
There is thunder in my bag that rocks the earth.
There is lightning in my bag that lights the heavens.
There is a boat in my bag that sails the angry sea.
There are fishermen in my bag who sail the boat.
There is a man in my bag who sleeps through it all.

The story

Our story takes place on a dark blue cloth…	*Place bag and smooth*
the colour of an angry sea at night. But to begin with, all is calm.	
A boat sails on the calm sea.	*Place the boat on the bag*
Inside are a group of friends.	*Place disciples in boat*
At the back of the boat a man sleeps.	*Place Jesus lying down*
The friends work the oars…	*Indicate rowing with your hands*
but still the man sleeps.	*Finger on lips: 'Shhhhh'*
The boat sails on.	*Move boat a little*
The friends quietly pull the oars.	*Make rowing movement*
They feel secure behind the boat's wooden walls. In the back of the boat, the one who made the seas sleeps…	*Finger on lips: 'Shhhhh'*
tired out by giving and loving, worn out by teaching and healing.	

You will need
- ✤ A dark blue bag
- ✤ 5 'people':
  4 disciples,
  1 Jesus
- ✤ A boat (cut down
  a box to make it
  shallow; attach a
  card boat shape
  to one side)
- ✤ (For thunder
  noise) A baking
  tray and wooden
  spoon
- ✤ A rain stick or
  shaker
- ✤ (For wind noise)
  A tube to swirl,
  or a plastic bottle
  to blow across *or*
  pupils' voices
- ✤ (For lightning)
  A torch

Reproduced with permission from *Bible Storybags*® published by BRF 2011 (978 0 85746 073 8) www.barnabasinschools.org.uk

THE MONSTER (THE STORM ON THE LAKE)

Older pupils

Suddenly the wind starts to blow...	*Make wind noises*
the sky darkens and rain begins to fall.	*Use rain stick*
Thunder rocks the earth...	*Make thunder noises*
and lightning flashes, lighting up the little boat...	*Switch torch on and off*
all alone on the deep, dark sea.	

A storm!	*Repeat storm noises more loudly*

A sudden storm,
a wild storm,
a monster of a storm!

The wind slaps the lake...	*Make wind noises*
lashing the water into huge waves.	*Bunch up cloth to make waves*
The boat that had seemed so secure is battered by the storm and tossed on the waves.	*Rock the boat*
Higher and higher goes the boat as it is lifted on the crest of the waves...	*Lift boat high*
then down, down on the other side.	*Plunge it down*
The walls that seemed so strong now feel like a nutshell on a vast sea.	

Whirled in the tempest...	*Make waves come over the side of the boat*
rocked by the storm...	*Rock boat*
the boat begins to sink. But the one who made the seas sleeps on.	*Finger on lips: 'Shhhh'*

Outside the boat, the monster roared.	*More storm noises*
Inside the boat, its master slept.	*Finger on lips: 'Shhhh'*

Reproduced with permission from *Bible Storybags*® published by BRF 2011 (978 0 85746 073 8) www.barnabasinschools.org.uk

THE MONSTER (THE STORM ON THE LAKE)

The friends are frightened...   *Indicate disciples*

their hearts melt in fear,
so they wake the man who sleeps through the storm.
He speaks words into the wind.   *Stand up Jesus*

The storm ceases...   *Smooth bag slowly,*
                                       removing waves

coming to heel at its master's voice.
The monster storm is muzzled by his power.

In the silence after the storm...   *Use finger to draw a*
                                           question mark in the air

questions hang in the air.
Who is he?
What power is this?

Questions
(See also page 11.)

✪ Who is the
   sleeping man?
✪ Why is he
   described as the
   one who made
   the seas?
✪ Why is the storm
   described as a
   monster?

Reproduced with permission from *Bible Storybags®* published by BRF 2011 (978 0 85746 073 8) www.barnabasinschools.org.uk

THE MONSTER (THE STORM ON THE LAKE)

The light

The healing of the blind man

Using the storybag® in Assembly

To introduce the subject, talk about things we can see, and play 'I spy'. (Be sensitive to any visually impaired children present.) Discuss favourite sights: you could display images of them on the projector. Ask pupils to share their favourite 'sights' (the things they would most miss if they could not see them).

With older pupils, explore different types of blindness, such as the blindness created by prejudice (not being able to see the good in people). For example, if we say, 'X is a horrible person', this shows that we might be 'blind' to X's good qualities. (**NB**: Take care over who you choose as an example, and arrange it beforehand.) Introduce the Bible story (see Introduction, page 7).

Present the story using the storybag® or the web version (see pages 103–105) and the biblical material (see page 101).

> **Comment**
> This is a story about light and different types of blindness. The blind man is healed of his physical blindness but others have a different type of 'blindness'. Some people may be able to see the sun and moon but they cannot recognize goodness when they see it. They are 'blinded' by prejudice and hatred. Jesus calls himself the light for the world, which is about Jesus coming to bring the light of God's love.

Reflection

Use the images of favourite 'sights' as a visual focus while children think of their own favourite 'sights' and, if they wish, say 'thank you' for them.

Prayer (optional)

Thank you, Father God, for a beautiful world that we often take for granted. Thank you for the gift of sight. Help us never to be 'blinded' by hatred or prejudice.

Using the storybag® in RE

Introduce the subject using some of the material from the assembly introduction (see page 100).

Select the appropriate script and turn to pages 9 and 10 to find ways of using it.

Biblical material

John 1:4–9; 8:12; 9:1–41

One day, Jesus was walking along when he saw a blind man begging. Jesus healed the man's eyes and the man went home seeing. The neighbours were amazed, because he had left home completely blind! 'It can't be the same person,' they said. 'It must be someone who looks just like him.'

'No, it's me,' said the man, and he told them what had happened. Everyone was stunned by his story so they took the man to the religious leaders and the man told them what had happened.

'The person who healed you must be a bad man,' said the religious leaders. 'He healed you on a holy day, which is against the law.' They sent for the man's parents and asked them what had happened.

The parents were frightened by the religious leaders, so they said, 'This is our son and he has been blind since he was born, but now he can see. We don't know how he came to see or who did it. Ask our son: he is old enough to speak for himself.'

'All I know,' said the man, 'is that I was blind and now I can see! I've already told you what happened. The man who healed me can't be a bad man. He has healed my eyes and that's a good thing, and good things come from God.' At this, the leaders got very angry and threw him out.

Jesus heard what had happened to the blind man, so he talked with him about different types of blindness. He explained that there is such a thing as blindness to goodness and right, as well as not being able to see. Jesus said that he was the light for the world. He had come to shine a light on wrong and to bring the light of God's love.

> **Note:** For a comment on this story, see the assembly section (page 100).

Follow-up activities

(See also pages 11 and 12.) Select from these activities according to the age and aptitude of your pupils.

1. Create a display of this story. Divide the board diagonally and place midnight blue backing paper on one half and silver on the other. Add two-dimensional versions of the items from the bag. Add questions and comments from the pupils.

2. Use thought and speech bubbles to express the thoughts and feelings of the characters. Add them to your display. Discuss what this story has to say to people today about the 'darkness' of prejudice and hatred.

3. The blind man had been blind since birth. What do you think he would have noticed first when he was able to see? What would have seemed strange to him? What would have delighted and surprised him? What is your favourite 'sight'? What would you most miss not seeing?

4. Explore the Christingle service and how it relates to Jesus as the light for the world. The websites listed below are active at the time of writing.

- www.request.org.uk > main site > festivals > Christmas > Christingle
- www.childrenssociety.org.uk > get involved > Christingle

5. Look at the painting *The Light of the World* by Holman Hunt (www.rejesus.co.uk > expressions > faces of Jesus). Explore images of this story and encourage pupils to express their own understanding through art.

- www.nationalgallery.org.uk > search 'Duccio' or 'man born blind'
- www.biblical-art.com > biblical subject > New Testament > Gospels, Jesus, public ministry: miracles
- www.biblepicturegallery.com
- www.Jesusmafa.com > mini posters

Drawing on what they have learnt, pupils can create a banner that will communicate the meaning of the metaphor 'the light for the world'. The banner could be displayed in a local church.

7. Draw round several pupils (with feet together) on the back of wallpaper. Place the figures around the room and label them as the main characters from the

biblical story. Inside the outlines, the pupils can write what they have learnt about each person from the story and script. The story is then enacted, or pupils can watch the teacher presenting the story again. They then add anything new they have learnt about the characters' thoughts and feelings, inside the character outlines. Outside the characters, they can write what other people thought or felt about them, what influenced them, and what pressures were on them. Use this exercise to extend the pupils' understanding of the story and to add depth to dramatic portrayals.

Symbols used in this story

- Light: Jesus as the light for the world. Light is also a symbol of insight—a different type of 'sight'. A light bulb above a person's head is often used (in cartoons, for example) to indicate a moment of insight.
- Darkness or night: blindness; also a symbol of lack of insight. (**NB**: make sure that darkness and night are never linked to ethnicity.)
- The 'others': the religious leaders who were opposed to Jesus. These people lived in the 'darkness' of prejudice.

Reflective activity

Jesus called himself the light for the world. Christians believe that he brought the light of God's love. He also called people to be like lights and show God's love to others. Place a large dish of damp play-sand in the middle of a circle of children. Put a PE hoop around it that children must not cross. Place one large white candle in the centre of the sand. Talk with children about how they can 'shed the light of love', and ask them for practical ways in which they could do it. Every time a child suggests something, the teacher lights a small birthday candle and adds it to the sand. (Have lots of different colours available so that children can choose.) If appropriate, light the smaller candles from the larger one, explaining that the large candle represents Jesus, and Christians believe that people can get the strength to love from Jesus.

Assessment

Assess the pupils' understanding by observing them replaying the script, or ask them to talk about the display or write about it.

Background information and understanding the story

For information on healing miracles, see page 89.

Jesus called himself the light for the world. Christians and people of Jewish faith use light as a symbol of God. Light shows the way, as a torch does. Light brings comfort in the dark, as a lamp or candle does. Light shows up wrong, as a security light in a shop does. Light warns of danger, as a lighthouse does.

The religious leaders insinuated that Jesus was bad. As the blind man pointed out, good things come from God and Jesus had done something good. Jesus' behaviour did not indicate that he was motivated by evil, but the leaders could not 'see' that. They had a different type of blindness.

The man's parents were afraid because the religious authorities were very powerful. People often thought that illness was a person's own fault or the fault of their parents. Jesus denied that this was so.

Jesus was accused of healing on the sabbath. Generally, no work was done on the sabbath, but 'acts of mercy' were allowed. Jesus often broke the strict sabbath rules out of compassion. He said, 'People were not made for the good of the Sabbath. The Sabbath was made for the good of people' (Mark 2:27).

Useful websites

The website listed below is active at the time of writing.

- www.textweek.com/art/art.htm > Jacob to Mustard Seed > Jesus/Christ > Healing

Script 1

Unpacking the bag

My bag is silver, for this is a story about light.
There is midnight blue in my bag, the colour of night.
There is a man in my bag who never sees the light.
There is a man in my bag who is the Light.
There is a sun in my bag that lights the day,
and a moon and stars that light the night.

The story

Our story starts on a silver cloth, for this is a story about light *(place bag and smooth)*. It is also a story about darkness, so we cover some of the light with a dark cloth *(place blue cloth over half the bag)*.

This is the man who lives in darkness *(place blind man on the blue cloth)*. His eyes have never seen the sun *(hold up sun; place on blue cloth)*. His eyes have never seen the moon *(hold up moon; place on blue cloth)*. His eyes have never seen the stars *(hold up stars; place on blue cloth)*. He lives without light, for he is blind.

This is the man who is called 'the Light' *(place Jesus on silver bag)*. He came to bring light to the man who lived in darkness, so that he could see the sun, see the moon and see the stars *(hold up sun, moon and stars in turn and place on silver cloth)*. The man who was 'the Light' healed the eyes of the man who lived in darkness and spread the light of love wherever he went *(move Jesus to stand next to blind man)*. The man who once lived in darkness now lives in the light *(move blind man and Jesus to the silver side)*. Now he can see the sun, see the moon and see the stars *(hold up sun, moon and stars in turn and place on blue cloth)*.

You will need
❖ A silver bag
❖ A midnight blue cloth
❖ Paper sun, moon and stars
❖ 2 'people': 1 blind man, 1 Jesus

Questions
(See also page 11.)

❂ Why is one man called 'the Light'?
❂ Why does the other man live in darkness?
❂ How is love like a light?

Reproduced with permission from *Bible Storybags*® published by BRF 2011 (978 0 85746 073 8) www.barnabasinschools.org.uk

THE LIGHT (THE HEALING OF THE BLIND MAN)

You will need

* A silver bag
* A midnight blue cloth
* Paper sun, moon and stars
* 2 'people':
  1 blind man,
  1 Jesus
* 2 extra 'people'

Script 2

Unpacking the bag

My bag is silver, the colour of light.
There is midnight blue in my bag, the colour of night.
There is a man in my bag who lives in darkness.
There is a man in my bag who is the Light.
There are others who live in a different darkness.
There is a sun in my bag that gives light to the day.
There is a moon in my bag that gives light to the night.
There are stars in my bag that stud the sky.

The story

Our story starts on a dark cloth…	*Place blue cloth*
for this is a story of darkness. Our story ends on a silver cloth…	*Place silver bag, then cover half with blue cloth*
the colour of light where no shadow falls. On one side stood a man who lived in darkness.	*Place man on blue cloth*
On the other side stood a man who is the Light.	*Place Jesus on silver side*
Between them stood people who lived in a different darkness.	*Place others on blue cloth*
The man who lived in darkness had never seen the sun…	*Lift and place sun on blue cloth*
had never seen the moon…	*Lift and place moon on blue cloth*
had never seen the stars.	*Lift and place stars on blue cloth*
In his world of night no light shone.	
Into his darkness came the Light…	*Place Jesus on blue cloth*
and one man's world of night ceased.	*Move Jesus and man to silver cloth*
Now he could see the sun…	*Lift and place sun on silver cloth*

Reproduced with permission from *Bible Storybags®* published by BRF 2011 (978 0 85746 073 8) www.barnabasinschools.org.uk

THE LIGHT (THE HEALING OF THE BLIND MAN)

now he could see the moon…	*Lift and place moon on silver cloth*
now he could see the stars…	*Life and place stars on silver cloth*
that God made.	

But others stayed in night: theirs was a different darkness.	*Lift and replace other people*
They could not 'see' the Light, although they could see the sun…	*Lift and place sun on blue cloth*
see the moon…	*Lift and place moon on blue cloth*
see the stars that God made.	*Lift and place stars on blue cloth*

The Light shone in the darkness…	*Hold up Jesus*
and the darkness could not put it out.	

Questions
(See also page 11.)

- Who lives in darkness?
  Who is the Light?
- Who can see in this story?
  Who is blind?
- Is there more than one type of sight?
- Is there more than one type of blindness or darkness?

Reproduced with permission from *Bible Storybags®* published by BRF 2011 (978 0 85746 073 8) www.barnabasinschools.org.uk

THE LIGHT (THE HEALING OF THE BLIND MAN)

The small man

Zacchaeus

Using the storybag® in Assembly

To introduce the subject, change your appearance by putting on a hat, a different jacket and so on. You could bring a range of clothes and let the children change your appearance. Give yourself a different name or let the children give you a different name. Explain that some changes are easy to make (clothes, name) but others are very difficult. Today's story is about a difficult type of change—a change in behaviour and attitudes. Introduce the Bible story (see Introduction, page 7).

Present the story using the storybag® or the web version (see pages 109–112) and the biblical material (see page 107).

> **Comment**
> This is a story about change and making amends: change from loneliness to friendship; change from greed to giving; change from rejection to acceptance. It's a story about freedom, about no longer being trapped by selfishness and greed. With older pupils, explain how Zacchaeus had ruined his life by his behaviour; it was as if he had forged a chain that bound him.

Reflection

Have a silent reflective time in which you hold up, one at a time, items from the bag and ask pupils to think about what they have heard.

Prayer *(optional)*

Teacher: *For times when we hurt others through greed and selfishness...* (hold up crowd)

All: *Forgive us, Lord.*

Teacher: *For times when we hurt ourselves through greed and selfishness...* (hold up Zacchaeus)

All: *Forgive us, Lord.*

Teacher: *Free us from selfishness and any wrongs that hinder us from serving you and others...* (Hold up Jesus)

Introduce the subject using some of the material from the assembly introduction (see page 106).

Select the appropriate script and turn to pages 9 and 10 to find ways of using it.

Biblical material

Luke 19:1–10

Zacchaeus was a tax collector who lived in the town of Jericho. The people hated him because he collected money for the Romans, the enemy. The people also hated Zacchaeus because he took too much money from them—money they needed for their families.

Jesus was on his way to Jericho and the word quickly got round. People began to gather by the road, waiting for him to arrive. Zacchaeus, like the others, wanted to see Jesus but he was a short man and he could not see over the heads of the crowd. No one would let him through, and the only view Zacchaeus was likely to get was of people's backs. Standing there all alone, he thought about his life. He had lots of money but no friends. Zacchaeus had heard about Jesus and wanted to see him, but how could he if no one would let him through?

Then Zacchaeus remembered the tree. He tucked his tunic into his belt and began to climb. He could hear people laughing at him but he didn't care. When he got to the top, Zacchaeus sat on a branch. He could see right down the road. In the distance he saw Jesus. He kept watching as Jesus drew closer and closer. When Jesus reached the tree, he stopped, looked up at Zacchaeus and said, 'I must stay at your house today.'

Zacchaeus was stunned. So were the people. They began to mutter, 'Why stay with a tax collector? He's a greedy thief.'

Zacchaeus climbed down the tree and went home with Jesus, and from that moment he changed. He offered to give back four times the amount he had stolen, and anything he had left over he would divide in two and give half to the poor.

Note: For a comment on this story, see the assembly section (page 106).

Follow-up activities

(See also pages 11 and 12.) Select from these activities according to the age and aptitude of your pupils.

1. Create a display on a bright green background, adding two-dimensional versions of the items from the bag. A three-dimensional tree can be made using corrugated card and tissue. Add questions and comments from the pupils.

2. Draw two thought bubbles and write on them the thoughts of the crowd and Zacchaeus at the beginning of the story. Using different coloured bubbles, write the thoughts of the crowd and Zacchaeus at the end of the story. How have they changed? What caused the change? Discuss with the pupils what causes them to change. Add some bubbles to the display.

3. With older pupils, discuss the chain metaphor. Sometimes people do things that create guilt in themselves and bad feelings in others. This can be like carrying a heavy weight or chain around. Forgiveness is like breaking the chain. Pupils can create chains from strips of coloured paper. Write key words on the links, describing the sort of things that become like a chain, and add the chains to the display.

4. Divide pupils into groups of seven. The groups discuss what would have been going though Zacchaeus' mind when he heard that Jesus was coming. After this, six people in each group form lines of three, facing each other (as in a barn dance). These people will act as Zacchaeus' mind and will speak his thoughts, so they need to think through what they will say. The seventh pupil in each group represents Zacchaeus. She or he walks slowly between the lines as the others speak Zacchaeus' thoughts. The person representing Zacchaeus literally 'collects his thoughts'. When the class comes back together, the people representing Zacchaeus report on his state of mind. Discuss with pupils the idea of listening to our thoughts and the promptings of conscience.

5. Mime the story. Before you start, discuss the story and its message, as the mime needs to communicate this message. Break the story into key episodes, then locate key movements and gestures. Join them together to form the whole story. Evaluate the mime.

6. Explore how artists express their understanding of this story, and encourage pupils to do the same. The websites listed below are active at the time of writing.

- www.biblical-art.com > biblical subject > New Testament > Gospels, Jesus, public ministry: encounters
- www.sermons4kids.com > art by Henry Martin, scroll to PowerPoint slides
- www.Jesusmafa.com > mini posters

Symbols used in this story

- The chain: the guilt and wrong that the small man carries.
- Green and yellow: spring colours, used to symbolize new life.
- Scarred hands: Jesus the carpenter who knew what it was like to live as an ordinary person. Also a symbol of the scars of the crucifixion, which Christians believe to have been a battle between good and evil, where Jesus defeated wrong, showing that he was strong enough to set people free.

Reflective activity

With younger pupils, in circle time talk about how greed and selfishness can make people lonely. Pass around a sad face while doing this. Talk about putting things right and having a fresh start.

With older pupils, spend some time in quietness, thinking about the things that spoil friendships while passing a paper chain (see activity 3). Discuss how invisible 'chains' can be broken.

In church schools, it may be appropriate to hang the chains over a cross. Explain that Christians believe that Jesus came to break the chains of wrong (sin) and sadness. Pupils can then remove the chains, break them and lay them at the foot of the cross.

Assessment

Assess the pupils' understanding by observing them replaying the script, or ask them to talk about the display or write about it.

Background information and understanding the story

This is a story about rescue. The word 'salvation' means rescue. Jesus' name means 'God rescues' (saves). Zacchaeus is rescued from himself and the sin (wrong) that ruined his life.

It is also a story about 'repentance', which in Hebrew means 'a change of direction'. Zacchaeus' life changed direction.

Zacchaeus was a tax collector who collected money for the hated Romans—the people who had invaded the country—so tax collectors were seen as collaborators. Zacchaeus was a chief tax collector, which probably means that he was quite wealthy. The Romans allowed tax collectors to collect money on top of the taxes to pay their own salary. Some collected a lot more than they were allowed.

Most people lived close to the poverty line, so a bad harvest or increased taxes could have terrible effects.

Useful websites

The websites listed below are active at the time of writing.

- www.theway2go.org > the hub > yellow ball > the taxman
- www.textweek.com/art/art.htm > Salome to Zechariah > Zaccheus

Script 1

Unpacking the bag

My bag is green, the colour of new life.
There is a road in my bag, and a tree for climbing.
There is money in my bag for taking and giving.
There is a man in my bag who takes but learns to give.
There is a crowd of people who hate the man.
There is a teacher in my bag who helps the man whom everyone hates.

The story

Our story takes place on a bright green cloth *(place bag and smooth)*. It is the colour of new leaves. Across the cloth runs a road *(place ribbon)*. This is the road that runs through the town. Beside the road is a tree *(place tree)*, making a cool and shady place. Lots of people stand beside the road *(add crowd)*; they are waiting for the teacher. Behind them stands another man, a small man *(place small man)*. He is small and cannot see over the crowd *(jump him up and down)*. No one will let him through *(shake head; move small man back one pace)*. Everyone hates him, for he is greedy and selfish. No one will talk to him *(shake head; move him back a pace)*. No one will be his friend *(shake head; move him back a pace)*. He is lonely.

Along the road comes the teacher *(place Jesus on road)*. Everyone wants to see him *(indicate crowd)*, but the small man cannot see anything so he decides to climb the tree *(place small man in tree)*. From his hiding place in the branches, he can see the teacher *(hold up Jesus)*. To everyone's surprise, the teacher stops beneath the tree *(place Jesus under the tree)* and tells the small man to come down *(take small man out of tree)*. 'I am coming to your house,' says the teacher.

The crowd feels angry *(indicate crowd)*. 'Doesn't he know that this man is bad? He is a greedy, selfish person who takes other people's money' *(drop coins on cloth)*. The teacher and the small man leave *(move them away from the crowd)*. We do not know what the teacher said *(shake head)*, but the small man came out of his house *(bring small man forward)* and told the people that he was giving back all the money he had taken and much, much more *(gather crowd around him)*! The people could not believe it at first, but they did believe it when the small man visited their houses giving back their money *(drop coins)*. A new life started for the small man—a new life where he was no longer lonely, a new life where he had friends.

Reproduced with permission from *Bible Storybags®* published by BRF 2011 (978 0 85746 073 8) www.barnabasinschools.org.uk

THE SMALL MAN (ZACCHAEUS)

You will need
* A bright green bag
* A yellow ribbon for the road
* A cardboard tube with screwed-up green tissue pushed in at the top for leaves (snip both ends of the tube and bend out the card to make it stand, and to make a platform for Zacchaeus at the top)
* 6 'people': 4 crowd, 1 Jesus, 1 small man
* A few coins

Questions
(See also page 11.)

* Who might the teacher be?
* Why is the small man lonely?
* Why do people hate him?
* How did the small man change?

You will need
* A bright green bag
* A yellow ribbon for the road
* A cardboard tube with screwed-up green tissue pushed in at the top for leaves (snip both ends of the tube and bend out the card to make it stand, and to make a platform for Zacchaeus at the top)
* 6 'people': 4 crowd, 1 Jesus, 1 small man
* A few coins
* A small chain made from paper links

Script 2

● Unpacking the bag

My bag is green, the colour of new life.
There is a road in my bag that leads to freedom.
There is a tree in my bag for someone to climb.
There is a man in my bag who takes and gives.
There is money in my bag that is taken and given.
There is a crowd in my bag who hate the man.
There is a chain in my bag that is heavy and hard.
There is a rescuer in my bag who breaks chains.

● The story

Our story takes place on a bright green cloth…	*Place bag and smooth*
for this is a story of new life. Across the cloth runs a road.	*Place road*
It is the road to freedom. Beside the road stands a tree, ready for climbing.	*Place tree on far side of road*
This is the story of a small man…	*Place small man in one corner*
an unhappy man, a man who was not free, a man who had much and little. He had much money…	*Drop coins*
but little love and few friends.	
The small man limped along the road dragging an invisible chain.	*Hold up chain*
Each link he had forged himself…	*Move small man a little*
links of greed and selfishness. Each link was as hard as steel…	*Point to links*
as hard as his heart.	

Reproduced with permission from *Bible Storybags®* published by BRF 2011 (978 0 85746 073 8) www.barnabasinschools.org.uk

THE SMALL MAN (ZACCHAEUS)

A crowd gathered along the road. *Place crowd*

They heard the small man coming.
They always heard, and got out of his way.
Turning their backs, they ignored him,
for they hated him.
This was the man who took what little they had.
They were used to the clanking of his chains. *Hold up chain*

Each link had been formed by their misery and tears.

The small man limped on... *Move the small man*
behind the crowd

dragging his chain behind him.
He was small on the outside... *Hold up small man*

and small on the inside,
for goodness had shrivelled inside him
like a dying plant. *Point to your chest*

Suddenly the noise of the crowd
drowned the noise of his chain.
The Rescuer had come... *Place Jesus at start of road*

the one who set people free.
The small man strained to see the Rescuer... *Move small man nearer*

but all he saw was the backs of those
who hated him. *Jump him up and down*

Seeing a tree close by, he decided to climb. *Climb tree slowly*

The chain dragged with its weight,
each step was painful and slow,
but the small man longed to be free, so he climbed on.

Resting on a branch, the small man watched. *Sit small man in tree*

The Rescuer was gentle
but his hands were strong and scarred—
the hands of a workman.
Were his hands strong enough to break chains... *Lift chain*

Reproduced with permission from *Bible Storybags*® published by BRF 2011 (978 0 85746 073 8) www.barnabasinschools.org.uk

THE SMALL MAN (ZACCHAEUS)

chains as strong as steel?
The Rescuer stopped beneath the tree.
He looked up and smiled at the small man,
calling him down.   *Place Jesus beneath tree*

In shocked silence the crowd watched.   *Bring small man down*

In a quiet place, the Rescuer...   *Place small man and Jesus*
                                                    together, away from crowd

broke the chains with his scarred hands,
and set the man free.   *Break chain*

Now when the small man walks...   *Move small man across bag*

no chain warns people of his coming...   *Hold up broken chain*

no weight drags him down...   *Turn crowd to face him*

he no longer limps through life.
He is still small on the outside,
but inside love grows like a watered plant.   *Group crowd around him*

The small man is no longer small.
The small man is no longer alone.
This is the man who gives where once he took.   *Add coins*

Questions

(See also page 11.)

❂ Who might the
Rescuer be? Why
is he called this?

❂ What are the
chains? How was
the man set free?

❂ Why is the road
called the road
of freedom?

Reproduced with permission from *Bible Storybags®* published by BRF 2011 (978 0 85746 073 8) www.barnabasinschools.org.uk

THE SMALL MAN (ZACCHAEUS)

The purple story

The crucifixion

Using the storybag® in Assembly

To introduce the subject, talk about times when we are sad. Use a puppet or persona doll if possible. What makes people sad? Use another puppet or doll to explore the idea of being ashamed. What does 'ashamed' mean? Explain that today's story is a very sad story. It also has in it some people who are ashamed. Introduce the Bible story (see Introduction, page 7).

Present the story using the storybag® or the web version (see pages 117–120) and the biblical material (see page 114).

Comment

This is a story of hatred, shame and sadness that are eventually turned to forgiveness, hope and joy. The image of tears and blood turned to diamonds and rubies is used. It's about love and forgiveness turning negative things (hatred, sadness, shame and death) into something positive (joy, hope and new life). Emphasize that this is not the end of the story. Christians believe that Jesus rose to new life, showing that love is stronger than hate, and life is stronger than death. His death was a beginning of joy, hope and new life.

Reflection

Set up a table with a purple cloth, a cross and a white candle in a simple bowl of damp play-sand as a reflective focus. Light the candle at the start of the assembly and blow it out at the moment when Jesus dies in the story.

Explain that this is a sad story but it is also a story of hope (hold up a rainbow ribbon, if used). Sometimes, when we are sad, we find it difficult to believe that things can change. This story says that love has the last word: it is stronger than hate and evil.

Prayer (optional)

Thank you, Father, that the story of Good Friday reminds us that love, forgiveness and hope are powerful weapons that can change the world.

Introduce the subject using some of the material from the assembly introduction (see page 113).

Select the appropriate script and turn to pages 9 and 10 to find ways of using it.

Biblical material

Mark 15:16–41; Matthew 27:32–55; Luke 23:26–49; John 19:17–37

For the betrayal by friends, see Mark 14:10–11, 43–50, 66–72. See also Psalm 23:4: 'the valley of the shadow of death' (RSV).

Jesus was all alone. His enemies had sent soldiers to arrest him and all his friends had run away and left him, just when he needed them. One of his friends, Judas, had told Jesus' enemies where to find him. Another, Peter, had denied he even knew Jesus. It was a sad and terrible day.

Jesus was taken to court, but the witnesses made up lies and they could not agree on their story. He was taken to the Roman judge called Pilate. Pilate knew that Jesus was innocent and tried to let him go, but the crowd called for the death penalty. Only a few days before, this same crowd had welcomed Jesus to Jerusalem.

Jesus was beaten and the soldiers made fun of him, putting a crown of thorns on his head and a cloak on his shoulders. They blindfolded him and said, 'If you are a king, tell us who hit you.' Jesus remained silent. He never fought back.

Jesus walked to his death carrying his cross, and people lined the streets. Some friends and followers watched, unable to believe that such a good man could be about to die. As Jesus was dying, he found time to comfort a thief who was also dying, and he asked God to forgive the people who had hurt him.

For his friends, family and followers, it felt like the end. But this is only part of the story. It was not the end—it was the beginning of the beginning.

Important note: For a comment on this story, see the assembly section (page 113). This reminds children that this is not the end of the story and introduces the idea of resurrection.

Follow-up activities

(See also pages 11 and 12.) Select from these activities according to the age and aptitude of your pupils.

1. Encourage pupils to listen to music as they reflect on the story. They can express their own ideas and understanding through sound and music. For example, use Barber's *Adagio* for a dance to express the sadness of Good Friday. Fabric can be used as an extension of the dancers' bodies. Discuss what colours would be appropriate.

☸ *Adagio for Strings* by Barber
☸ 'In tears of grief' from *St Matthew Passion* by Bach
☸ *Adagio in G Minor* by Albinoni

2. Create a display on a purple background, adding two-dimensional items from the bag. Sections of the script can be used to caption the display. Add pupils' questions and comments.

3. Create a sad face from a paper plate and add sticky dot 'tears'. Use this as a stimulus to discuss being sad or sorry (keep the discussion general and anonymous) and why the friends were sad in the story. Use a second face with the dots rearranged to form a smile. Use this as a stimulus to talk about Good Friday and how forgiveness, love and hope can turn sadness and shame into joy. Add these faces to the display.

4. Follow up the symbols in the script in art, exploring their meaning. Make rainbows and tears in different media. Use the symbols to create a Good Friday banner for a local church—for example, silver and red 'drops' arranged around a cross on a purple background. Add a rainbow as a symbol of hope or colour the cross in rainbow colours.

5. Write the story of Good Friday from the point of view of the road, in either prose or poetry. What would the 'song of the road' be? Think about what the road would have witnessed. What do you think it would say?

6. Explore how artists express their understanding of this story. Select images with care, avoiding distressing images; choose appropriate images for the age of the

pupils. Georgia O'Keeffe's *Black Cross, New Mexico* can act as a model (available on the CD *Cracking Easter*, from www.stapleford-centre.org). Pupils can make a class 'stained-glass' window using translucent paper. Arrange two strips of black paper as a cross and stick them to the paper, cutting off surplus paper from the cross (see diagram). Colour the paper to suggest hope, and display on a window.

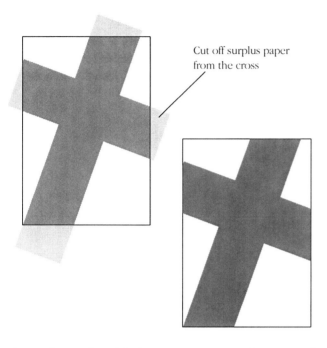

Cut off surplus paper from the cross

The websites listed below are active at the time of writing.

- www.nationalgallery.org.uk > search 'crucifixion'
- www.biblical-art.com > biblical subject > New Testament > Gospels, Jesus: passion
- www.mccrimmons.com > posters > seasonal > Easter
- www.jesusmafa.com > posters or mini posters
- www.heqigallery.com (browse galleries)

A gallery of Easter images and activities appropriate for schools can be found on the CD *Cracking Easter*, available from www.stapleford-centre.org. Church schools may be interested in the pack *Experience Easter* for use in partnership with a local church. Visit: www.gloucester.anglican.org/education/resources > educational publications

Symbols used in this story

- Cross: the crucifixion; where Christians believe Jesus conquered wrong (sin).
- Crown of thorns: a suffering king; mockery.
- Road: the journey through life. The end of life can also be a beginning (life after death).

- Diamonds and rubies: tears and blood. Sorrow and sin are turned into something beautiful by love, forgiveness and hope.
- Rainbow: a sign of promise, hope and a new beginning.
- Setting sun: death, but also a promise of the new dawn (resurrection).

Reflective activity

With older pupils in church schools, cover a table with a purple cloth and add a caption: 'Easter is about forgiveness'. On the table, place two small baskets containing large beads, both silver (or clear) and red. The beads should be the large 'thread-on' variety. If you can't find beads, chop up some large party straws in appropriate colours. On the table, place plastic laces that will go through the beads. If they wish, pupils can spend a few moments thinking about the story and adding a red and silver bead to a 'necklace'. When they add a silver bead, they can think about being sorry. When they add a red bead, they can think about forgiveness. In church schools the lace can be hung over a cross.

With younger pupils, or in community schools, pupils can make a memory bracelet. Cut a strip of thin card and make slits at either end (see diagram). Decorate with silver sticky dots arranged in a slight arc as a reminder of tears and smiles. Talk about how sorrow and regret can be turned into joy by forgiveness, love and hope.

Slit

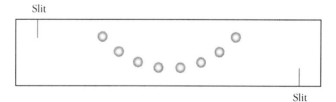

Slit

Assessment

Assess the pupils' understanding by observing them replaying the script, or ask them to talk about the display or write about it.

Background information and understanding the story

Christians describe the crucifixion as a battle between good and evil. In this battle, love and life won: Jesus took all the hate that the world could throw at him and even died for those who hated him. Christians believe that Jesus triumphed over evil and death when he rose from the dead, showing that love and life are stronger

115

than sin and death. Go to www.theway2go.org > the hub > yellow ball > crossfire to see a Christian understanding of the cross.

Crucifixion was a form of execution kept for slaves and criminals. Jesus was crucified with two criminals, but Jesus himself had been declared innocent by Pilate, who judged the case in court. Prisoners had to carry the crossbeam of the cross, not the whole cross: the upright was kept at the execution site.

Jesus was buried on Friday, before sunset, as the Jewish religion insisted that all bodies should buried before the sabbath, which began at sunset. He was given a tomb by a follower called Joseph of Arimathea. The tomb would have been like a cave, with a stone in front of it.

NB: This story deals with death and needs handling very sensitively, particularly with young children. Pastoral concerns should be uppermost.

Useful websites

The websites listed below are active at the time of writing.

- www.reonline.org > infants > festivals > Easter
- www.request.org.uk (browse teacher's area)
- www.topmarks.co.uk > search 'Easter'
- www.textweek.com/art/art.htm > Jacob to Mustard Seed > Jesus/Christ > Crucifixion
- www.theforgivenessproject.com > stories (the story of Michael Watson might be suitable for older pupils: it shows the inspiration of Jesus' example in forgiving on the cross)

Script 1

Unpacking the bag

My bag is purple, the colour of sadness; the colour of a king.
There is a road in my bag that leads to a cross.
There is a king in my bag who is loved by some and hated by others.
There are people in my bag who cry for the king.
There are others who do not.
There is a rainbow in my bag, a sign of hope.

The story

Our story takes place on purple, for this is a story of sadness *(place bag and smooth)*. It is also the story of a king, for purple is the colour worn by kings. Across the cloth runs a road *(place road)*. At the end of the road is a cross *(place cross at the end of the road)*. At the side of the road stand some friends. They are crying because they are losing a king who was their friend *(place two people and add some 'tears' to the bag)*. On the other side are more friends. They are crying because they did not help the king when he needed them. They feel ashamed *(place two more friends and add more 'tears')*. At a distance stand some enemies. They are not crying; they hate the king *(place two more people)*.

Down the road comes the king *(place Jesus at the beginning of the road)*. He walks to the cross. It is here that he will die *(walk Jesus to the cross and stand him in front of it)*. He dies for the friends who love him *(lift one set of friends)*. He dies for the friends who did not help him *(lift the other set of friends)*. He dies for the enemies who hate him *(lift the enemies)*. He loves friends and enemies alike, for this is the king of love *(indicate Jesus)*. He forgives them all.

All the people go home *(remove all but Jesus)*. The king is taken to a quiet garden, where he is laid to rest *(remove Jesus)*. As the sun sinks in the sky, the terrible day ends *(indicate sinking sun with hand gesture)*, but this is not the end. As the suns sets, its rays catch the tears and, for a few seconds, a rainbow is formed *(add rainbow)*. Something beautiful is about to happen.

You will need
❖ A purple bag
❖ A light brown ribbon for the road
❖ 7 'people': 4 friends, 2 enemies, 1 Jesus
❖ A cardboard cross on a stand, or a small wooden cross
❖ Silver paper tears
❖ A rainbow ribbon or rainbow paper

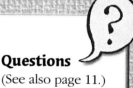

Questions
(See also page 11.)

❶ Why are people crying?
❷ Why do you think some people hate the king?
❸ I wonder what is about to happen?

Reproduced with permission from *Bible Storybags®* published by BRF 2011 (978 0 85746 073 8) www.barnabasinschools.org.uk

THE PURPLE STORY (THE CRUCIFIXION)

Script 2

You will need

* A purple bag
* A light brown ribbon for the road
* 7 'people': 4 friends, 2 enemies, 1 Jesus
* A cardboard cross on a stand, or a small wooden cross
* Silver paper tears
* Red shiny paper droplets
* A crown of thorns (twist tissue paper into a circle with points)

Unpacking the bag

My bag is purple, the colour of sadness; the colour worn by kings.
In my bag, there is a road that leads from nowhere to everywhere.
It is the road to the end.
There is a crowd in my bag, weeping.
There are friends in my bag, crying.
There are tears in the bag that fall like diamonds.
There are soldiers in my bag—the execution squad.
There is a cross in my bag that must be carried.
There is a crown of thorns in my bag that is worn by a king.
There is blood in my bag, as red as rubies.

The story

Our story takes place on purple…	*Place bag and smooth*

the colour of a bruise, for this is a story of pain.
Our story takes place on purple…
the colour of royalty, for this is the story of a king.

Across our cloth, like a scar, runs a road…	*Show the road*
the road that leads from nowhere to everywhere…	*Place road on cloth*

the road to the end.
It is a dark and shadowy road, narrow and bare.

The road is empty, except for a cross…	*Place cross at end of road*

that casts its shadow over the road.

Beside the road stands a crowd, noisily weeping.	*Place two people*
Their tears fall to the ground like diamonds.
They are burdened with grief…	*Place a few tears on the bag*

for they are losing a leader,
the man who is all alone.

Reproduced with permission from *Bible Storybags*® published by BRF 2011 (978 0 85746 073 8) www.barnabasinschools.org.uk

THE PURPLE STORY (THE CRUCIFIXION)

On the other side of the road stand the friends,
silently crying.   *Place two more people*

their tears mingle with the dust.
They are heavy with shame…   *Add more tears to bag*

for they have betrayed their friend,
the man who is all alone.

Soldiers step on the road…   *Add two soldiers
                                    to the start of the road*

their boots ringing on the hard-packed earth…
crushing tears beneath their feet. *Use the flat of your hands
                                    to make boot sounds*

They are untouched by the sadness of the crowd.   *Lift crowd*

They do not notice the crying friends.   *Lift friends*

They are the execution squad.   *Move soldiers to the cross*

Then comes the man who is all alone.   *Place the Jesus at the
                                       start of the road*

He looks around.
He is touched by the sadness of the crowd…   *Lift crowd*

who grieve for him.
He is touched by the shame of his friends…   *Lift friends*

who have betrayed him.
He is touched by the hardness of the soldiers…   *Lift soldiers*

who trample tears beneath their feet,
and he is silent.

The man who is all alone steps on to the road.   *Use hands to indicate the
                                                  sound of feet on the road*

The sound echoes down the valley of the crowd,
the valley of shadows.
He has started his journey…   *Move Jesus down road*

on the road that leads from nowhere to everywhere,
the road to the end.

Reproduced with permission from *Bible Storybags*® published by BRF 2011 (978 0 85746 073 8) www.barnabasinschools.org.uk

THE PURPLE STORY (THE CRUCIFIXION)

On his head he wears a crown of thorns,
thorns that cut and bite and scar.
From his head great drops of blood fall...

Add red drops to bag

as rubies at his feet.
He carries his crown to the cross...

Place crown of thorns on cross

and there he dies.

Stand Jesus in front of cross

As the sun sets, its rays light up the earth,
and in the dying sunlight it looks as if...

Lift 'tears and blood' and let fall

it glistens with diamonds and rubies.
Something is about to happen.

The man who is all alone has reached
the end of the road.

Run finger down road and off cloth

It is the road to the end,
that is also a beginning.

Questions
(See also page 11.)

- Who is the man who is all alone? Why is he all alone?
- Where does the road lead? What does it mean?
- Why was the man betrayed?
- How can an end be a beginning?

Reproduced with permission from *Bible Storybags®* published by BRF 2011 (978 0 85746 073 8) www.barnabasinschools.org.uk

THE PURPLE STORY (THE CRUCIFIXION)

The beginning

The resurrection

Using the storybag® in Assembly

To introduce the subject, talk about times when sadness is changed to happiness. Draw a sad face on a paper bag and give your paper-bag puppet a name. Ask the pupils why the puppet is sad and give them some options to choose from. Pop a larger paper bag over the top with a smiley face. What might have happened to make the puppet happy? Explain that today's story is about a change from sadness to happiness. Introduce the Bible story (see Introduction, page 7).

Present the story using the storybag® or the web version (see pages 124–126) and the biblical material (see page 122).

Comment

This is a story about grief and sadness being changed to joy. For Christians, it is the most important story of all, because it tells of Jesus' resurrection. Christians believe that Jesus rose from the dead and came back living and loving. They believe that this shows that death is not the end and that life and love are stronger than hatred and death. Christians believe that Jesus is still alive and can be an invisible friend.

Reflection

Hold up items from the story for the reflection, making a short comment on each one.

Alternatively, ask every child and member of staff to wear something gold-coloured or bright yellow to assembly as an expression of joy and celebration—for example, yellow socks, gold coloured scarf, or gold coloured sticky badges (which can be made in class beforehand). Have a gold cloth and white candle as a reflective focus. Play joyful music.

Prayer *(optional)*

Thank you, Father, that at Easter we can celebrate the victory of life over death, and good over evil, through the death and resurrection of Jesus.

Using the storybag® in RE

Introduce the subject using some of the material from the assembly introduction (see page 121).

Select the appropriate script and turn to pages 9 and 10 to find ways of using it.

Biblical material

Mark 16:1–8; Matthew 28:1–10; Luke 24:1–12; John 20:1–18

After Jesus died on the Friday, some friends took his body and wrapped it and placed it in a tomb, like a cave. A large stone was rolled in front of the tomb and sealed. The family and friends then went home to mourn. All day Saturday they stayed together, sharing their sorrow. It was the holy day: nothing could be done.

On Sunday morning, several women walked to the tomb, taking spices with them to place on the body. It was a final act of kindness for their friend. On the way, they wondered how they were going to roll away the stone: it was large and heavy. The women walked quietly on, each thinking their own thoughts. Jesus had been their friend, their leader, the one who brought hope for the future. Now he was gone.

Nearing the end of the road, the women looked up. To their amazement, the stone was already rolled away and there, sitting on one side, was an angel. The women became afraid but the angel said to them, 'Don't be afraid. Jesus is not here; he is risen from the dead. He is alive again. Go and tell the others.'

The women did not know what to think. They ran back down the road to tell the others. This had been an amazing day—the day of all days.

> **Note:** For a comment on this story, see the assembly section (page 121).

Follow-up activities

(See also pages 11 and 12.) Select from these activities according to the age and aptitude of your pupils.

1. Encourage pupils to listen to music as they reflect on the story. They can express their own ideas and understanding through sound and music.

- 'Easter Hymn', from *Cavalleria Rusticana* by Mascagni
- 'Long live God' from *Godspell* by Schwartz
- Modern Easter music and songs used in worship (available from Christian bookshops)

2. Choose some of the music to develop an Easter dance. Communicate through movement the change from sorrow to joy. Pupils can evaluate the dances. How far did they express the events and emotions of the Easter story? What makes people joyful today? How is their joy expressed?

3. Create a display of the story by covering a board in gold paper and adding two-dimensional versions of the items in the bag. Use parts of the script as captions. Add questions and comments from the pupils.

4. Discuss why this is the most important story for Christians. Explore how it is celebrated at Easter and interview Christians concerning its relevance to them.

5. Create an Easter poster or card for a church entitled 'The beginning…'. You can use some of the symbolism from the story (gold, flowers and so on).

6. Explore how artists express their understanding of this story, and encourage pupils to do the same. The websites listed below are active at the time of writing.

- www.nationalgallery.org.uk > search 'resurrection'
- www.biblical-art.com > biblical subject > New Testament > Gospels, Jesus: resurrection and ascension
- www.biblepicturegallery.com.
- www.mccrimmons.com > posters or banners > seasonal > Easter
- www.jesusmafa.com > posters or mini posters
- www.heqigallery.com (browse galleries)

Easter images, activities and lesson plans can be found on the CD *Cracking Easter* available from the website www.stapleford-centre.org. See also *A-cross the World* by Martyn Payne and Betty Pedley for crosses from different cultures (BRF, 2004). Church schools may be interested in the pack *Experience Easter with Children* for use in partnership with a local church: www.gloucester.anglican.org/education/resources . educational publications

Symbols used in this story

✪ Gold: heaven and celebration.

✪ Grey: sorrow.

✪ Tears: sadness.

✪ Flowers: new life.

✪ Grave-tomb: loss of hope and loss of life; a prison for both.

✪ Open mouth of tomb: freedom; life let loose from the bounds of death; hope.

Reflective activity

With older pupils, talk about new beginnings and hope. Add flowers made from tissue paper and art straws to a vase while suitable music plays. In church schools, pupils can make a large cross from card and cover it with elastic bands (not too tightly). To appropriate music, each child can add their own paper flower to the cross (slotting it into an elastic band). Time can be spent thinking about new beginnings and hope.

With younger pupils, make gold 'happiness' badges to wear. In circle time, discuss what changes sadness to happiness. Link this discussion to the story, if appropriate.

Assessment

Assess the pupils' understanding by observing them replaying the script, or ask them to talk about the display or write about it.

Background information and understanding the story

Jesus died on the Friday afternoon and was buried before the start of the Jewish sabbath, which lasts from sunset on Friday to sunset on Saturday. The women would not have been able to visit the tomb until daybreak on Sunday.

Easter is the most important festival for Christians because it is the time when they celebrate Jesus rising from the dead. Christians believe that Jesus died, then rose again, showing that death was not the end and evil does not triumph. They believe that in some way Jesus' death and resurrection broke the power of sin and death. This belief gives Christians hope for life now and for the future. For more on Christian beliefs about the resurrection, see www.theway2go.org > the hub > yellow ball > Alive!

The women who went to the tomb had followed Jesus and supported him throughout his ministry. Jesus had female as well as male followers (Luke 8:1–3) and these women stayed with him while he was dying and noted where he was buried. The women took with them sweet-smelling spices, which were traditionally put on the body at burial. The women had been unable to do this before as the burial had been hasty. They had come to pay their last respects.

Jesus was buried in a rock tomb (a cave). A large stone would have been placed over the mouth of the cave.

Useful websites

The websites listed below are active at the time of writing.

✪ www.reonline.org.uk

✪ www.request.org.uk (browse teacher's area)

✪ www.topmarks.co.uk > search 'Easter')

✪ www.textweek.com/art/art.htm > Jacob to Mustard Seed > Jesus/Christ > Resurrection

Younger pupils

You will need

✂

* A gold bag
* Grey ribbon for the road
* Silver paper tears
* 4 'people': 3 women, 1 angel
* A circular margarine tub with separate lid for the grave-tomb (both covered in brown tissue)

Questions
(See also page 11.)

* Why are the women crying?
* How was sadness changed to joy?
* Why is it called 'the day of all days'?

Script 1

Unpacking the bag

My bag is gold, the colour of joy.
There is a road in my bag that is grey, the colour of sadness.
There is a grave-tomb in my bag that is closed with a stone.
There are women in my bag who are sad, for they have lost a friend.
There are tears in my bag, for the women are crying.
There is an angel in my bag who brings good news.

The story

Our story starts on a gold cloth, the colour of joy, for this is a story of sadness turned to joy *(place bag and smooth)*. Across our cloth runs a grey road *(place road)*. It ends in a grave-tomb *(place closed tomb)*. Along the road walk three women *(place women on road)*. The women cry as they walk. They are sad, for their friend has died *(sprinkle some tears)*.

Slowly the women walk along the road *(move women)*, but when they reach the grave-tomb they find the stone door open *(open tomb)*. An angel stands at the tomb *(place angel)*. The angel brings a message of good news. The friend they thought was dead is alive! The women run down the road to pass the message on *(move women quickly down the road)*. This is a joyful day, the day of all days.

Reproduced with permission from *Bible Storybags*® published by BRF 2011 (978 0 85746 073 8) www.barnabasinschools.org.uk

THE BEGINNING (THE RESURRECTION)

Script 2

You will need
- ❖ A gold bag
- ❖ Grey ribbon for the road
- ❖ Silver paper tears
- ❖ 4 'people':
  3 women,
  1 angel
- ❖ A circular margarine tub with separate lid for the grave-tomb (both covered in brown tissue)
- ❖ Paper sun
- ❖ Small paper or silk flowers

Unpacking the bag

My bag is gold, the colour of glory.
There is a road in my bag, a road of sadness.
There is a tomb in my bag that is sealed with a stone.
There are tears in my bag that flow freely.
There are people in my bag who shed tears.
There is an angel in my bag who speaks of living.
There is a sun in my bag that warms the earth.
There are flowers in my bag that burst into life.

The story

Our story takes place on gold; the colour of glory.	*Place cloth and smooth*
Across our cloth runs a grey road.	*Place road*
It is a dead, dry road where nothing grows. It is a road of tears that ends at a tomb…	*Sprinkle tears on road*
a cave whose mouth is stopped with a stone.	*Place closed tomb*
Feet walk the road, slow with grief.	*Use hands to make slow walking noises*
They carry their sadness in silence.	
This is the cave that swallowed the life they loved.	*Indicate tomb*
This is the tomb that ends all possibilities; that imprisons hope.	
For a day the road is silent.	*Finger on lip*
No feet walk there…	*Shake head*
no tears water it.	*Brush aside tears*
Only the sun bakes its hard…	*Hold up sun, then place on cloth*
dry surface where nothing grows.	

Reproduced with permission from *Bible Storybags®* published by BRF 2011 (978 0 85746 073 8) www.barnabasinschools.org.uk

Older pupils

Early one morning, women's feet
quietly walk the road...

Place women

and the smell of spices fills the air.
The women walk slowly...

Move them slowly

for grief weighs heavy.
Their tears water the ground.

Sprinkle tears on the road

The morning sun warms the road,
and beneath the ground seeds begin to grow,
watered by the women's tears and the
warmth of the sun.

Lift and replace sun

Soon the road will be covered in flowers.

The women reach the tomb...

Move women to tomb

but the mouth is open...

Roll away door

the stone is rolled away.
An angel speaks of living.

Place angel by tomb

Confused and excited,
the women run back down the road.

Move women quickly

Out of breath, they pause and look back.

Pause, look back

The cave stands open like a singing mouth.
The prison door gapes.
The life they loved has escaped...

Sprinkle flowers down the road

and with it hope is loosed into the world.
Anything is possible.
It is the beginning...

Questions
(See also page 11.)

- ❂ Who was 'the life they loved'?
- ❂ How does the tomb imprison hope and end all possibilities?
- ❂ The story ends with the words, 'It is the beginning...'. The beginning of what?

Reproduced with permission from *Bible Storybags*® published by BRF 2011 (978 0 85746 073 8) www.barnabasinschools.org.uk

THE BEGINNING (THE RESURRECTION)

Enjoyed
this book?

Write a review–we'd love to hear what you think. Email: reviews@brf.org.uk

Keep up to date–receive details of our new books as they happen.
Sign up for email news and select your interest groups at:
www.brfonline.org.uk/findoutmore/

Follow us on Twitter @brfonline

By post–to receive new title information by post (UK only), complete the form below and post to: BRF Mailing Lists, 15 The Chambers, Vineyard, Abingdon, Oxfordshire, OX14 3FE

Your Details

Name _____

Address_____

_____

Town/City _____ Post Code _____

Email _____

Your Interest Groups (*Please tick as appropriate)

☐ Advent/Lent   ☐ Messy Church

☐ Bible Reading & Study   ☐ Pastoral

☐ Children's Books   ☐ Prayer & Spirituality

☐ Discipleship   ☐ Resources for Children's Church

☐ Leadership   ☐ Resources for Schools

Support your local bookshop
Ask about their new title information schemes.

Lightning Source UK Ltd.
Milton Keynes UK
UKOW022259200412

191170UK00006B/1/P